The New Balanced Literacy School

Implementing Common Core

by Margaret Mary Policastro
and Becky McTague

Foreword by
Camille Blachowicz

The New Balanced Literacy School: Implementing Common Core
By Margaret Mary Policastro and Becky McTague

Cover Design: Sarah Bennett
Book Design: Jodi Pedersen

Credits:
Front cover photos: Dreamstime/Monkey Business Images (top), Capstone Studio (bottom)
Back cover photo of Margaret Mary Policastro by Bob Coscarelli

Library of Congress Cataloging-in-Publication Data

Cataloging-in-publication information is on file with the Library of Congress.
978-1-62521-629-8

Maupin House publishes professional resources for K–12 educators. Contact us for tailored, in-school training or to schedule an author for a workshop or conference. Visit www.maupinhouse.com for free lesson plan downloads.

Maupin House Publishing, Inc. by Capstone Professional
1710 Roe Crest Drive
North Mankato, MN 56003

www.maupinhouse.com
888-262-6135
info@maupinhouse.com

Printed in the United States of America in Eau Claire, Wisconsin.
032014 008094

Dedication

This book is dedicated to our beloved colleague and friend Richard "RJ" Ostry, who passed away on September 25, 2013. Richard was the assistant director in the Office of Community Engagement at Roosevelt University. His dedication to our work in the schools both inspired us and propelled us forward on a daily basis. Richard was the man working behind the scenes for us in many of the photographs in this book. It was his hard work that helped to create the spaces that are featured. He was a man of honor truly dedicated to all of his work. He loved going to the schools and watching his creative ideas unfold. Richard's support of our work will forever be cherished. We dedicate this book to RJ and his life at Roosevelt University, which will always be remembered.

Acknowledgments

We are very fortunate to be able to write about our passion: creating balanced literacy schools. There are so many people that we have gratitude and appreciation for in the process of writing this book. Last April on the way to the International Reading Association (IRA) in San Antonio, Margaret was delayed at O'Hare International Airport in Chicago and, by chance, met Nancy Stetzinger from Capstone. Nancy was quite interested in our work and invited us to visit the Capstone booth the next day at IRA. This is where we met Lynnette Brent, the new senior product manager at Capstone. That meeting started a relationship that culminated in the creation of this book. We want to thank the Capstone team that we met by chance; we do believe in miracles. We also want to acknowledge Karen Soll, Capstone acquisitions editor, as she has so gracefully coached us through the writing process. Karen has magnificent editorial skills to motivate writers to the next stage—not an easy task.

We would like to acknowledge all the people who have supported our work from the initial kickoff of our grant, which has led to the writing of this book. First, we want to thank Roosevelt University and the Office of Community Engagement for the unending support of our work, including Dr. Teryl Rosch, John MacDougall, and Jeanne Barnas. Their collective efforts have resulted in our continued funding opportunities. We want to thank Dr. Charles Middleton, president of Roosevelt University, for his visits to the schools, remarks at workshops, and meetings with evaluators. We thank all the people at the Illinois Board of Higher Education (IBHE), including Rich Jachino, Dr. Lisa Hood, and Dr. Dianne Gardner, our state-appointed evaluators at Illinois State University. We also thank Dr. Leanne Kallemeyn and Dr. Diane Morrison, both from Loyola University and both external evaluators. It was Leanne who encouraged the use of photographs to document our work. Today we have more than 2,000 photographs and many videos of our work in action. We also want to acknowledge Dr. Peggy Meuller and the Searle Family Fund the early support of our work.

Our work and this book would not have happened without our partner schools, who have welcomed us into their community of learners with open arms. The principals and administrators from the Archdiocese of Chicago Catholic Schools and the Chicago Public Schools welcomed us into their buildings for our work: Barbara Rasinski, principal at St. Bede of the Venerable, Chicago, Illinois; Dr. Pam Sanders and Steve Taylor from the former Fermi Elementary School in Chicago; Carolyn Jones and Stephen Fabiyi from Perkins Bass School in Chicago; Maureen Aspell, principal at Christ the King School in Chicago; Frank Embil and Ms. LaWanda Bell from Woodlawn Elementary Community School in Chicago; Dr. Elizabeth Alvarez and Sean McNichols from John C. Dore Elementary School in Chicago; and David Wood, Pat Gatewood, and Julie Hoeppner from Our Lady of the Wayside School in Arlington Heights.

A critical acknowledgment goes to the Roosevelt University literacy coaches who work daily out in the schools to support our work at all of these wonderful partner schools. These include Barbara Dress, Marlene Levin, Melissa Marquino Peterson, Noreen Wach, and Diane Mazeski. In addition to being a coach, Diane Mazeski gets an extra acknowledgment for her work during the past 26 years in the Roosevelt University Reading Clinic, which has led to the new balanced literacy model she has dedicated her professional life to. These energetic coaches provide the scaffolding day in and day out to make our model work.

There are many Roosevelt University graduate students who participated in our clinical practicum, which is the summer reading clinic. During the summer of 2013, we piloted our model in their classrooms so we would be ready to take the model out into our partner schools in the fall. We are most grateful for their willingness to stand by us and take a risk with us. These students include Ellen Pape, Laura Ross, Natalie Danaher, Matthew Lewan, Beverly Britton, Jennifer Trygar, Janet Donne, and Shannon Hart.

We also want to thank Jorie Sutton, our graduate assistant at Roosevelt University, who has been on call for us since August 2013, collecting resources and checking our citations. Finally, we thank our families who have supported all of our work over many years and especially while writing this book.

Table of Contents

Foreword by Camille Blachowicz

One of the trickiest aspects of any new initiative is making sure the "baby" of established effective practices does not get thrown out with the "bath water" of innovation. In the title of this resourceful book, Margaret Policastro and Becky McTague clearly signal their intention to integrate what research and practice have established as exemplary reading instruction with the theoretical underpinnings of the Common Core State Standards. And they make good on that intention. Using every one of their many years of experience as teachers, clinicians, and professional developers, they connect what good educators already know with what's new in reading instruction.

The key to making this connection is their understanding of the role of language in all literacy learning. James Britton noted that "Reading and writing float on a sea of talk." Policastro and McTague emphasize the primacy of building a strong language foundation and using and extending it in every aspect of their plan for creating balanced literacy schools. From their discussion of language-driven balanced literacy in Chapter Two, to investigating the important language demands of texts in a variety of school libraries in Chapter Three, to their emphasis on rich dialogue with parents and school educational personnel in building school teams in the chapters that follow, language is the thread that unites their vision with that of the Common Core and makes each aspect they discuss NEW.

A simple example of how this focus changes everything is their re-conceptualization of word walls as language walls. As a vocabulary researcher, I understand the importance of capturing the right words to drive change in thinking and thought, "Language Walls! Brilliant! Perfect tweaking of a concept that is familiar to all with one that signals new thinking." They back up their beliefs with many such practical, classroom-tested examples of the importance of rich language use by students and teachers in developing literate minds and carry this throughout this informative, theoretically sound, interesting, and useful text.

Margaret Policastro and Becky McTague have given the gift of their own language to share with the reader the insights they have gained through years of successful collaboration in both urban and suburban environments with teachers, coaches, and administrators. It is a gift that will keep on giving to the students who are our most important collaborators.

Camille L.Z. Blachowicz, PhD
Co-Director of The Reading Leadership Institute
Professor Emeritus
National College of Education
National Louis University

Chapter One: Introduction

A balanced literacy umbrella model on display in a teacher resource room

Creating a New Balanced Literacy School with the Common Core State Standards

For the last 13 years, we have been working in both urban and suburban schools, assisting teachers and administrators in creating balanced literacy schools. Each summer for the past 26 years, we have worked in Roosevelt University's Summer Reading Clinic, developing a best practice model that now captures all of the elements for a new balanced literacy program. Our work in the clinic has informed our work in the schools. The confluence of work with teachers and children has evolved into a strong foundation for pedagogy. Our work in the schools has been both as consultants and as external partners through grant-funded projects. Most recently, our work in the schools has been supported by a federal grant for improving teacher quality through the Illinois Board of Higher Education (IBHE) which allows us to work in the schools side by side with teachers and administrators. This work influences all of our teaching and classes at the university.

Several years ago, we realized that the current model of balanced literacy would need to be re-conceptualized in order to meet the instructional demands brought forth by the Common Core State Standards (CCSS). These new standards have influenced virtually everything we do in literacy and literacy instruction. We have therefore been able to refine our work, over and over again, based on the observational data we have collected. Moreover, the instructional shifts necessary to implement the CCSS require a new way of thinking and decision making on the part of the teacher. Consequently, pedagogy changed in all of the instructional tenets of balanced literacy. This brought about the need for new balanced literacy approaches. Schools and districts striving to become balanced literacy driven will find many ideas in this book to assist and support the process.

The purpose of this book is to get you started on the continuum of creating a new balanced literacy school. We approach this endeavor from a school-wide perspective rather than that of individual classrooms and teachers. The success of a school requires enormous collaboration and capacity building through teams. For some, this resource may serve as an introduction, while others might find this to be a continuing point to move forward in a new balanced literacy community. Balanced literacy is an ongoing process that is guided by the decision making of the administration and each teacher as well as the collective decision making of the literacy and grade-level teams. Each chapter addresses specific areas for capacity building and creating the new balanced literacy school and poses guiding questions to think about. Space for writing notes and reflections, along with tools to guide you into the new balanced literacy, are also included. In essence, this book tells the story of how we have created balanced literacy schools (and now new balanced literacy schools). We hope it will serve as a personal journey in your own professional development and quest towards balanced literacy.

These main questions should be used as guideposts when getting started in creating or continuing a balanced literacy school.

- What is the definition of balanced literacy?
- How has balanced literacy evolved?
- What does a new balanced literacy school look like?
- What is a literacy team?
- How do grade-level teams function in a new balanced literacy school?
- How do you create multiple in-school libraries?

The New Balanced Literacy Model

Guiding Question:

- How does the umbrella model represent the new balanced literacy school?

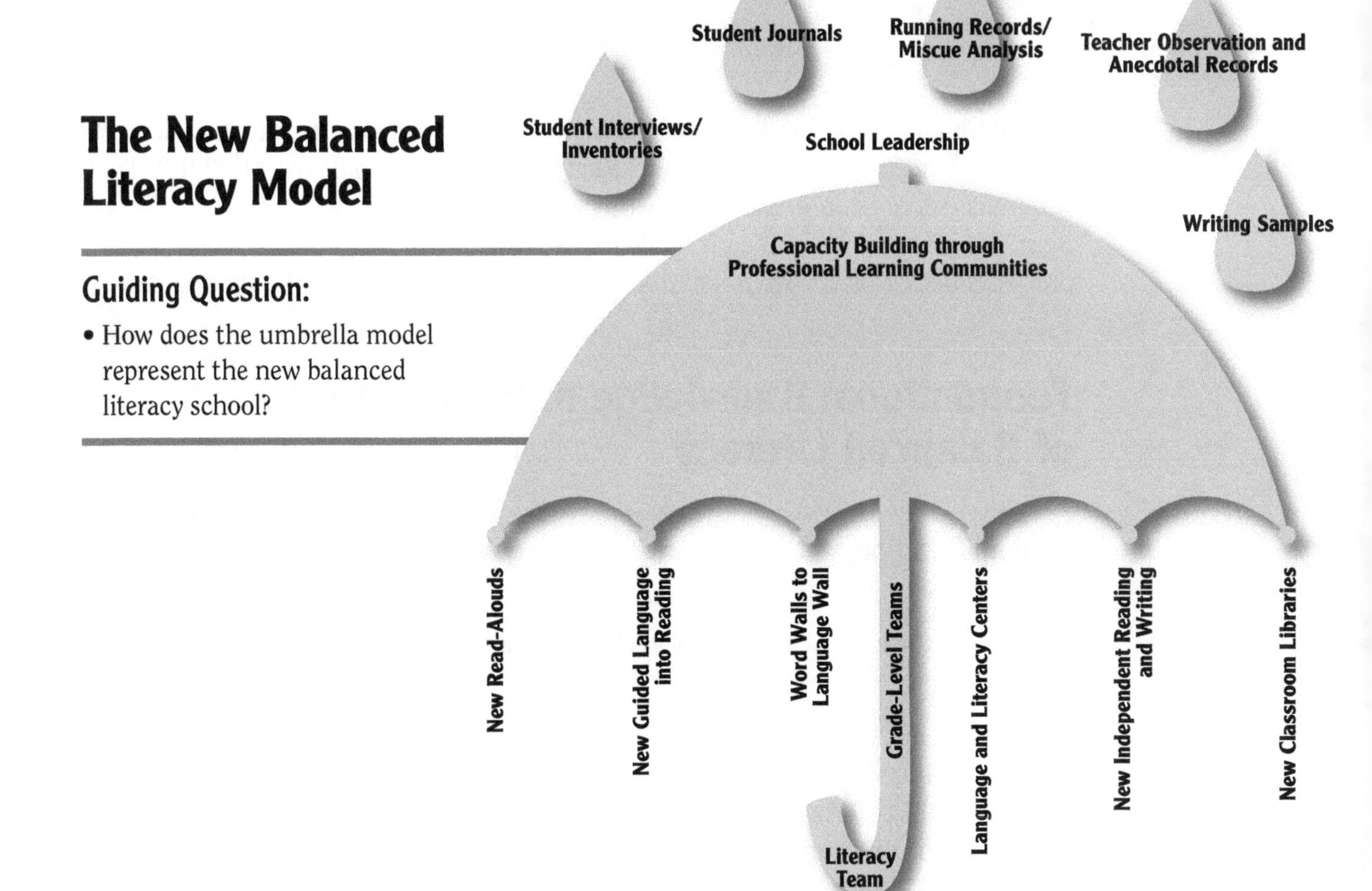

The new balanced literacy can be a complex and overwhelming topic for beginning teachers and those who are new to the concept. In order to present the information in an organized manner, the model using an umbrella is represented here. Rudell, Rudell, and Singer (1994) discuss a model as a metaphor to explain and represent complex theory. Unrau and Alverman (2013) discuss models in the broader literacy field as metaphors that represent abstract constructs that might be quite difficult to operationalize. Thus, the umbrella model grew out of our teaching with both pre-service and in-service teachers as a way to explain and organize complex information.

This umbrella image serves as a model for balanced literacy. The canopy represents the broad categories within reading and writing workshops where deliberate and purposeful decisions are made for differentiating instruction for each child. The tips of the umbrella represent the individual tenets or characteristics of balanced literacy, such as multiple in-school libraries, new read-alouds, new guided reading, word walls to language walls, and language and literacy centers. The top of the umbrella represents the leadership team, which includes the principal and other administrators responsible for the school. The handle of the umbrella holds the school organizational and structural tenets of balanced literacy, which include grade-level teams and literacy teams responsible for the school-wide implementation of the model. Raindrops represent the assessment components of the balanced literacy classroom. Assessments include both formal and informal measures. We usually use a transparent umbrella model to represent practices that go public. The clear umbrella is another aspect of the metaphor to move practices toward deprivatizing teaching, which is essential to capacity building in schools (NCLE, 2013). These umbrellas serve as an important way to communicate the ideas of balanced literacy. Some schools even hang the umbrella in the entryway to let visitors know of the best practices taking place. See Appendix D for a balanced literacy umbrella template.

Foundational Knowledge and Background of Balanced Literacy

Guiding Questions:

- What is the definition of *balanced literacy*?
- What does the new balanced literacy school look like?

Historically, balanced literacy is not a new concept, but rather has evolved from ideas of balanced approaches and instruction. The designation of balanced literacy originated in California in 1996 (California Department of Education, 1996; Honig, 1996; Asselin, 1999) and has a long history, which grew out of the reading wars and debates about how best to teach reading (Tompkins, 2013). Balanced literacy is a philosophical orientation that assumes reading and writing achievement are developed through instruction and support in multiple environments in which teachers use various approaches that differ by level of teacher support and child control (Frey, et al, 2005; Fountas and Pinnell, 1996). This philosophical orientation or perspective means that there is not one right approach to teaching reading (Fitzgerald, 1999), but rather a balanced approach to literacy development. The teacher makes thoughtful choices about the best way for students to become successful readers and writers (Spiegel, 1998).

Another viewpoint surrounding balanced literacy is that it centers on best practices, stays away from the earlier debates, and attempts to discuss best practices in a more flexible manner. That is, there are many independent aspects of literacy that must be simultaneously balanced (Madda, Griffo, Pearson, and Raphael, 2007). Most recently, Tompkins (2013, 2010) describes the balanced approach to instruction as "a comprehensive view of literacy that combines explicit instruction, guided practice, collaborative learning, and independent reading and writing."

Within balanced literacy, key components include the home and community, library involvement, structured classroom plans, read-alouds, guided reading, shared reading, and independent reading and writing (Fountas and Pinnell, 1996). In balanced literacy classrooms, teachers are constantly making thoughtful decisions about each child that combine best practice instruction with frequent opportunities for students to apply what they are learning in authentic literacy activities.

This could mean that when a teacher is working with a small group in guided reading, deliberate decisions about the needs of the children are taken into account. The teacher might work on decoding with some, fluency with others, and comprehension with all of the children through a combination of explicit instruction.

Understanding how children learn best and what instructional practices influence reading and writing must be considered as a basis for school-wide transformational change. According to Cohen and Cowen (2011), "The primary goal of a balanced literacy program is to teach reading not as a skill broken into isolated steps, but as a lifelong learning process that promotes higher-order thinking, problem solving, and reasoning." Learning theories that support a student-centered balanced literacy classroom include constructivist theory (Smith, 2004), sociolinguistics (Vygotsky, 1986), and cognitive/information processing (Tracey and Morrow, 2006).

Check out these websites on balanced literacy by searching for the following information online:

- Maya Angelou Elementary—Balanced Literacy Handbook: This guide lays out the components of balanced literacy, along with tips and explanations.
- The K-Crew's Website: This site includes lots of resources and information on best practices for balanced literacy.
- Carol Hurst's Children's Literature Site: Authors Carol Otis Hurst and Rebecca Otis talk about text selection to use in guided reading.
- Ms. Ross's First Grade Class: The Barrett Elementary Center teacher highlights literacy centers in her classroom.

Links to Language and Language Development

Guiding Questions:

- What is the connection between language and literacy?
- How does language guide all of our literacy instruction?
- What is classroom discourse?
- What about English language learners?

A rising challenge is the connection of language and language development and the important role it plays in all aspects of literacy and literacy instruction. Thought and language are intricately tied together and, as such, contribute to all aspects of the learning process. The new ELA Common Core State Standards require high levels of cognitive rigor that place new learning demands on students, requiring the highest levels of Bloom's Taxonomy for learning, and thus call for new insights and directions into the teaching and learning of these standards.

Halliday's (1993) language-based theory of learning captures the idea of making meaning as a semiotic process, i.e., the resource for making meaning is language. From this perspective, his general theory of learning is interpreted as "learning through language." Most importantly, intentionally **learning about language to inform all of literacy instruction** is critical for both teachers and school leaders entering into the implementation of the CCSS. Language from this perspective takes on many different forms. For example, one teacher in our clinic was reading the book *Flat Stanley* with her guided reading group and she began by asking the question "What does the word *bulged* mean?" This word was part of the next section they were about to read. Given the nature of Stanley and his flatness, this was a curious question. One student responded and said, "I think it is when you are running and you, like, bulge into something and it bulges out." Another student responded and said it is when something is "popping out." While she was responding, another student puffed up her cheeks with air to show them bulging out. The teacher then began to pinch her check and stretch it out while she was spelling "b-u-l-g-e-d." Important here is the language that took place during the response to the question. Language was clearly in action here, and it became apparent that the responses were constructed from more than just words. The actions of the students and the teacher helped to construct meaning and guide a response. The teacher took time for this discussion to happen and was patient as the group worked through a response together.

Paramount to student success is deliberately re-examining best practices in literacy instruction with a powerful new lens and shift of awareness to language development (which incorporates language as action, language and learning as social cognition and discourse, etc.). The term "discourse" is seen prominently in the academic language portion of the instructional shifts. Unfortunately, practicing teachers have had little preparation for this concept and are often unclear about the implementation of discourse into instruction. Gee (2001) defines "discourses" as the "ways of combining and coordinating words, deeds, thoughts, values, bodies, objects, tools, technologies, and other people so as to enact and recognize specific socially situated identities and activities." Classroom discourse typically refers to the language that students and teachers use to communicate with each other, including talking, discussions, conversations, and debates. Although this is a complex term to understand and put into classroom use, Rudell and Unrau (2004) explain that classroom discourse is about creating an abundance of oral texts the students and the teacher interpret. This interpretation of how to comprehend the message, the source of the message, and the truth or correctness of the message is central to classroom discourse.

These forms of discourse take on many different formats within the classroom setting and happen during large- and small-group instruction, along with students working in pairs, and are all paramount to all classroom conversations. Embedded within these rich conversations are the socially situated identities. Visiting a first-grade classroom recently, we saw the teacher had a word wall that had expanded to a language wall about rural versus suburban living. The children learned about these concepts, then developed a debate, and had to argue the merits of both. We asked this teacher if she would have considered introducing argument to her first graders a year ago before her professional development on CCSS and her response was "Never." Part of the ongoing and systematic professional development included rich and thoughtful discussions about what classroom discourse is and what it looks like in a classroom. This indeed has become a critical element in the preparation of both pre-service and in-service teachers.

With CCSS, classroom discourse demands that discussions revolve around rigorous argument supported by evidence. These discussions are public for other students to refute and debate with a persuasive evaluation. Teachers' roles and responsibilities within classroom discourse will change as they model, scaffold, and become facilitators of the discussions.

Teachers must know when it's just the right time to step into the discussion as well as when to back out and let the discussion be student-to-student led. In order to promote this type of social dialogue within the classroom, the environment must be safe and promote risk-taking. In one classroom in our clinic, we observed a teacher introducing debate to her second and third graders. She posed the question, "What is a debate?" A student responded by saying, "When two groups of people are against each other and they are telling a story or solving a problem. It doesn't mean you are against each other like me and Joseph. We are best friends and live across the street from each other. So it means that we just have different opinions and ideas about things." The shift of instruction here will call for greater amounts of class time for students to explain with evidence and less time with the teacher doing the talking. Setting up this class environment where students value all the ideas and opinions expressed in class will be critical. The shift in these types of instruction will emphasize students learning from students as the role of the teacher will be to talk less and facilitate more.

Both conversation and discourse are necessary for higher-level thinking and teaching. Teachers and school leaders need guidance on how to activate classroom discourse, how to know when it is happening, and how to use the opportunities to construct meaning and comprehension. They must also step back from current instruction to see the meta-language and metacognitive processes involved in this new knowledge of instruction and learning. Finally, teachers and leaders need to know how to guide language into literacy as a staircase of complexity—using language to inform, guide, and scaffold all instruction. These skills must be integrated to include close readings with informational and challenging texts, building student knowledge, and developing habits for evidentiary arguments through social discourse. Evidentiary argument is basically providing evidence for an argument. For example, if a student is doing research on the question of why fish in a particular lake are dying, the teacher can provide multiple texts for the reading lesson and research. The sources of text could include an opinion article from the newspaper, a climate report from the EPA, a National Weather Service climate report from 1900–2000, and a pollution report from a factory located on this particular river. Students would then need to find facts and evidence to support an argument on why the fish population is dying.

The new balanced literacy model reflects the critical and essential role that language plays in all areas of instruction. In all the tenets of the new model, we emphasize and highlight the importance of language. In the new read-aloud, there is an emphasis on awareness to the social discourse that takes place alongside the rich conversations. In the new guided reading, teachers are urged to have students' language guide instruction, with language acting as the scaffold and informing the instruction in literacy. Special attention is given to the development of academic language and social discourse. With the movement from word walls to language walls, the unit of study is now larger than simply a word and incorporates the situated discourse embedded within all instruction. This situated discourse happens during a reading lesson or any content-area lesson as the children and the teacher engage in conversations and discussions. These discussions can be teacher-led or student-to-student in large groups, small groups, and one-on-one. The new language and literacy centers are built around the idea that students now work in teams solving problems at centers where a social construction of knowledge and language is happening.

A traditional balanced literacy model can be effective and successful for instructing English language learners (ELLs) as well as struggling readers and students who need enrichment. However, the new balanced literacy model will support ELLs more effectively because language and social discourse are the foundation of all of the tenets. Many of the programs and models that have been used to work with ELLs have stressed culture and language, but by stressing language first and having the focus of culture through stories or books and authentic writing, students are able to have more opportunities to hear and use language and thus improve their literacy strategies and skills.

ELLs enter a school and especially a classroom at very different stages of language learning. We know that students who are learning a second language are at different stages of language learning. The new balanced literacy model incorporates language in most of its elements so that ELLs can have language instruction that is both explicit and implicit. Language is used in the new read-aloud and because language is the basis of this element, it allows children to hear and experiment with language in a non-threating manner. Most facets of the new balanced literacy model, like guiding language into reading, language and literacy centers, and word walls to language walls, all have language as the center of these routines. The majority of instruction and support that an ELL encounters is concentrated around language. In addition, these language interactions occur in many places, so a teacher may observe language interactions not only with the teacher but with peers. Teachers can note the progress of how students are learning the new language and create simple checklists like the one here that document these changes over time:

- Is the child taking in new language?
- Is the child imitating other children's language in class?
- Is the child starting or continuing to pretend to understand the language?
- Is the child using body gestures?
- Is the child starting or continuing to use words and phrases?
- Is the child starting to use longer phrases?
- Does the child appear to comprehend but not have the language to express ideas?
- Is the child using grammatical forms of speech that seem like his/her first language?
- Does the child use vocabulary but in its literal form?

Perhaps the biggest challenge for ELLs, and especially for teachers who instruct ELLs, is the problem that Cummins (1999) discusses, which is transitioning students from basic interpersonal communication skills (BICS) to cognitive academic language proficiency (CALP). With CCSS, this will be more critical because students will have to read, comprehend, and analyze more complex text and more text that is informational. Using routines that are language based will support the ELLs learning with more challenging text and also instruction with informational books.

To read more about the implications of language and language development, please search online for the Stanford University website, "Understanding Language: Language, Literacy, and Learning in the Content Areas," which strives to heighten teacher awareness of the essential role that language plays in the new Common Core State Standards and the Next Generation Science Standards.

What Does the New Balanced Literacy School Look Like?

Guiding Questions:

- What changes are needed to create a new balanced literacy school?
- What does the new balanced literacy school look like in terms of access to books for children, teachers, parents, and administrators?

The new balanced literacy begins with physical, organizational, and structural changes that take place within the school. The physical changes begin with the creation of multiple in-school libraries that provide access to books for children, parents, teachers, and administrators. These libraries are in addition to the school library and work with the school librarian. For schools that do not have an existing school library, the multiple in-school libraries provide much needed access to books. With budget cuts looming, we have seen school libraries with no librarian and often the library is shut down with little or no access to the books for children and teachers. Year-round access to books is a critical dimension for success to carry out the best practices necessary for CCSS implementation in balanced literacy schools. Multiple in-school libraries can include the following and are described in the pages that follow:

- Parent library
- Guided reading library
- Read-aloud library
- Novel sets library
- Professional development library
- CCSS exemplar and informational text library
- Hallbrary

The structural and organizational changes begin by initiating both a literacy team and grade-level team within the school. The formation of a literacy team allows for a specific priority to be given to literacy. Here is how one principal described her school's literacy mission: "I want literacy to scream off the walls in every classroom and hallway, and I want everyone to know that literacy is our main priority." Grade-level teams in schools with literacy as a priority set agendas that focus on student data and growth in literacy. Thus, the function or purpose of these school-wide teams is to form both organization and structure to support literacy. See Chapter Four for details on these teams. Additionally, ongoing and systematic professional development is embraced through school-wide capacity building and collaboration.

Fullan and Quinn (2012) define capacity building as the "process of developing the ability of the individual or organization to make the changes required to improve learning for all students by integrating the development of knowledge, skills, and commitments." They also explain that collective capacity building promotes teachers and administrators working with and learning from one another with a goal of improving student learning. Capacity building happens through deliberate and planned team collaboration in a learning community. See Chapter Five for more details on capacity building.

Schools that already have high-functioning literacy and grade-level teams can focus on multiple in-school libraries and professional development. These processes of change will take place in different ways in schools, depending on the existing organizational structures that are already in place. Appendix B has guiding principles to assist schools that are starting out.

In order to close the summer reading loss for children, we believe that year-round access to books is a critical dimension in literacy success. This access includes summer reading, which requires a thoughtful plan for summer reading initiatives (SRI) in the school. Therefore, our new balanced literacy framework begins with the notion of access to books as a central theme of this resource. By "access," we mean making it easy for parents, grandparents, caregivers, teachers, administrators, and all children to read books using readily available, multiple in-school libraries. For teachers in a new balanced literacy school, this is a critical dimension as easily accessed books are necessary to implement a daily read-aloud, guided reading, and so on. In the new balanced literacy school, there are physical and structural changes that must take place for a successful shift in instructional practices and capacity building. The physical changes that take place include the development of these multiple in-school libraries:

Year-Round Access to Books through Multiple In-School Libraries

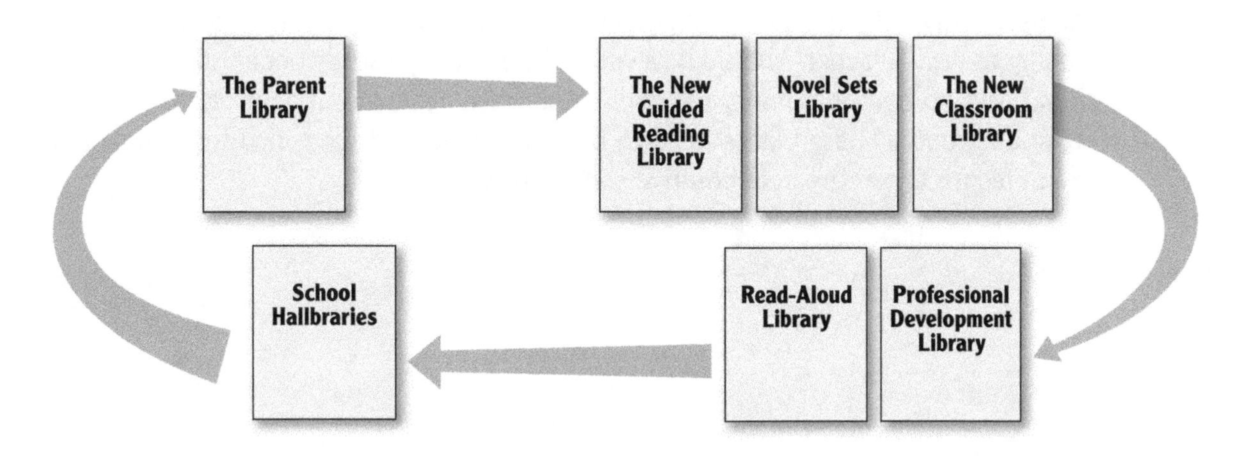

This model begins with the parent library, which is housed near the entryway in a school for easy access. It then moves to the access needed for teachers: guided reading for all, novel sets libraries in the upper grades, and all teachers having access to their own new classroom filled libraries. The arrows then move to the teachers and administrators to have access to professional development materials along with a collection of read-aloud favorites. The hallbrary is a new idea that has been developed to show how access to books in the new balanced literacy schools has no limits. The parent library is an equally important dimension for book access. Working with parents to develop family literacy and strong partnerships is both critical and essential for reading success. When parents have access to books, they are more readily able to provide books at home for bedtime story reading and family reading time.

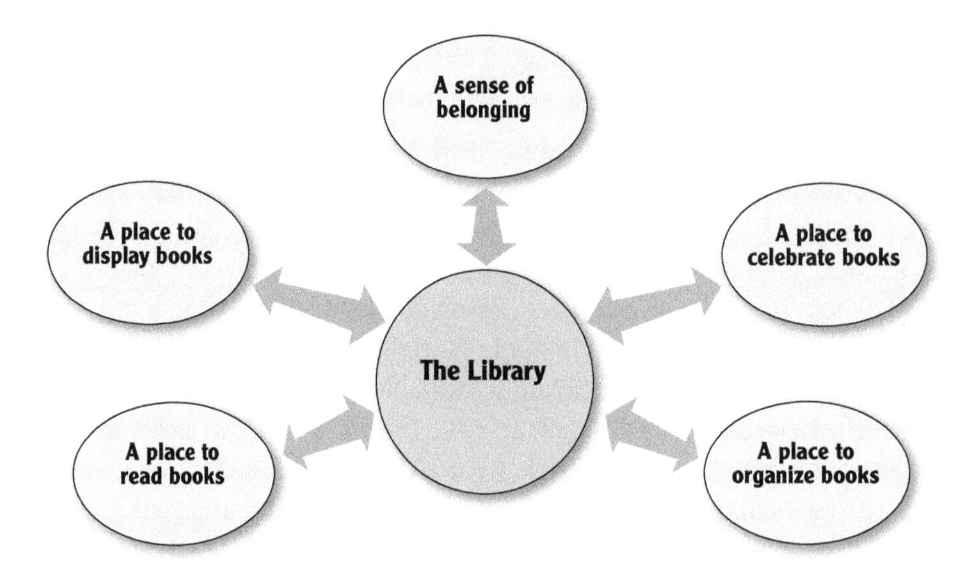

A library can provide an important sense of place in the multiple in-school libraries framework. A library can bring about feelings of belonging and the desire to return frequently. Libraries should provide a place where books are celebrated, and this should be reflected in the organization and structure of the individual library. Libraries should provide a cozy place for the reader to enjoy reading for any length of time, brief or extended. Libraries should be a place where books are displayed and the user is invited to pick up a book and read. This model of a library pertains to the teacher as well. Teachers should have an inviting place to study books, gather professional development materials, and collaborate with peers about good children's literature and more. These places need to be established and identified in schools and promoted for the entire collaborative community.

Photo Gallery of Physical Changes: Multiple In-School Libraries

The purpose of the photo gallery is to give you a snapshot of the evolution and development of the physical changes of libraries within a new balanced literacy school. This captures the essence of what libraries can offer. Each photo has dimensions of the framework model and shows access for the users, the collection range, variety, and a glimpse into how the library might be managed. Appendix A has more frameworks and checklists to assist in the process. Indeed, many questions about what things were like before the photo was taken may come to mind. Questions about how the actual libraries were created and other questions will percolate as you look at the photographs. The purpose is to give the reader ideas about how to create and construct school libraries that fit the building and the users within your population. Seeing some examples firsthand will hopefully provide ideas on how to begin or continue wherever you may be in the building and creation of libraries within your own schools.

The photos in this book represent a typical school day. Therefore, these are true snapshots of what a regular day looks like for a library. Neatness and tidiness were not a priority. Rather, when you can see books and stacks of books indicating that users are active in the selection process, the library is then serving its function and purpose. The library framework and models were developed and conceptualized after working for many years within schools. Having actual photographs to go along with a conceptual framework assists in the development and actualization of a library. In some sense, it is an attempt to begin to merge information about libraries and the best practice theories—a springboard for where you are—and it will help to bridge new adventures into multiple in-school libraries. Please see Appendix A for more information on setting up libraries.

The Parent Library

School **entryways** have inviting **parent libraries** (in the picture to the right, it is called the **family lending library**) to invite the community in to check out books. We want this community to include parents, grandparents, and caregivers. The parent library is a foundational library that can set the tone for the new balanced literacy school. When the school entryway is transformed into a space that creates access to books for the parents and the community at large, it sends an important message about family literacy and home and school partnerships. Creating a literate environment that includes the parents and community is critical for school-wide literacy success. The bridge between home and school is one that should be promoted and celebrated each school day. This happens by inviting parents and caregivers into a space that they can count on to gather books for home reading, which might include bedtime stories and daily read-alouds. The parent library is an equally important dimension for book access.

Working with parents to develop family literacy and strong partnerships is both critical and essential for reading success. When parents have access to books, they are more readily able to provide books at home for bedtime story reading and family reading time. In the new balanced literacy school, these parent libraries are rich with a variety of texts that allow parents to bring home informational and complex texts within all the content areas, including poetry.

The photograph to the right represents the space after the parent library was created. Before, the wall was black and dismal looking. With the removal of a black corkboard wall and the installation of bookshelves and a bench, the entryway was transformed, sending a welcoming message about literacy to the community.

For parents, several factors are important when considering the development of a library. First, it is important to place the library where parents can have easy access to the collection. It should also be user friendly so parents can feel comfort and ease in having access to books. Having the library open and available when parents drop their children off and pick them up is important. When parents come for meetings during the day and after school, the library should be available.

Beyond the entryways and the parent libraries, the new balanced literacy schools have multiple other libraries to support access to books for parents, children, teachers, and administrators.

Think about the entryway of your school and where the perfect place for a parent library could be.

For more information on parent libraries, see Appendix A and these references:

- Policastro, M., Mazeski, D., & McTague, B. (2010/2011). Creating the parent library: Enhancing family literacy through access to books. *Illinois Reading Council Journal,* 39(1).
- For information on reading aloud and free downloadable handouts for parents, please search the Internet for Jim Trelease's homepage.

New Read-Aloud Library

The new balanced literacy schools have a **read-aloud library** where teachers have easy access to daily read-aloud selections in their classrooms. Reading aloud to children takes on many different forms and formats. Typically, a read-aloud is when a teacher selects a book and orally reads it to a group of children. Reading aloud is appropriate for all grades (preschool through eighth) in an elementary school and is equally important for the upper grades as well. The read-aloud collection now has 50 percent informational texts in kindergarten through fifth grade and 70 percent in grades six through 12, including all content areas and poetry to align with the instructional shifts necessary to meet CCSS. In schools where best practices are encouraged and developed, easy access to a collection of read-aloud books makes the selection and securing of a daily read-aloud easier for all. The collection consists of books that have been favorites for both teachers and children. At this school, there is a commitment to reading aloud each day in every classroom.

This is a distinctive feature of a new balanced literacy school and enhances the use of best practices. The routine of a new, daily read-aloud is further supported when teachers have a collection aligned with the CCSS they can count on for their planning and instruction. A read-aloud library is also an indication of the unifying practices within the school; that is, best practices that are shared and made public in such venues as this display. This collaborative endeavor is also a major contribution to the overall capacity building in a new balanced literacy school. Please see Appendix A for more information on setting up a read-aloud library.

Where would you visualize a read-aloud library in your school?

Guided Reading Library

Balanced literacy schools have a **guided reading library** (housed in what is often referred to as the "book room" or "balanced literacy room"), where teachers have access to leveled books and materials. The new guided reading library should include a balance between fiction and nonfiction. The guided reading library in this school is a room where teachers gather for teacher meetings, parents meetings, and guest speakers. It's also where teachers eat lunch. This room has evolved over the years and now holds the guided reading collection. Access is vital for all primary-grade teachers who teach near this room. This room is bright, comfortable, and inviting for all users.

The guided reading library is one of the most essential of all multiple in-school libraries. Here the access to books becomes a critical factor in meeting the needs of all the children in the primary grades. When authentic, leveled texts can be placed in a central location for all primary teachers, easy access and usage issues are met. When teachers share and collaborate about their collections of leveled books and the range, levels, and variety of literature offered for the children, an ever-expanding opportunity for school-wide capacity building occurs. The guided reading library will also need to reflect the CCSS shift to more complex and challenging texts for students. Thus, re-leveling books to challenge students will be an important task for schools to take on. The literacy coach can assist in this task as well as the management of the collection, and the grade-level team can have discussions about usage and management as well. Please see Appendix A for more information on setting up a guided reading library.

Where do you visualize a guided reading library in your school?

Novel Sets Library

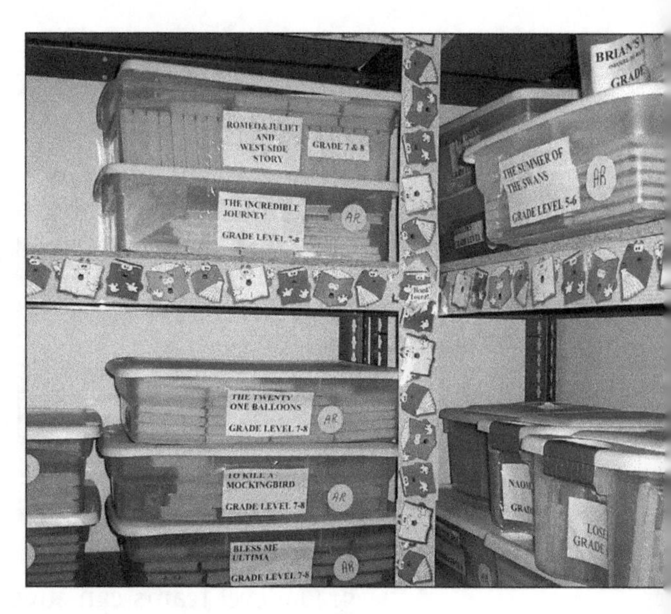

Balanced literacy schools have a **novel sets library**, which is sometimes housed along with the guided reading library in the "book room." The collection includes selections that are representative of the Common Core exemplar texts. Additionally, the novel sets collection consists of authentic literature, biographies, award-winning books, traditional literature, and young adult and graphic novels. Novels sets of 25 to 30 books are in large transportable bins and labeled with the title and range of grades for which the book is appropriate. Grade-level planning and school-wide capacity building can be enhanced when teachers have access and opportunities to plan for novels to be read throughout the year. This photo of the novel sets library shows the range and density of the collection. Although this room is not large—more like a big walk-in closet—it holds the bins on shelves that go from the floor to the ceiling. A creative border is added to the shelving, which makes the room feel inviting and appealing.

The photo shows the bins and labels with title and grade ranges. Each bin contains a class set of 25 to 30 novels, depending on the number of students in a classroom. Teachers should plan accordingly so they have access to bins that can be easily transported to their classrooms. When planning a novel sets library, it becomes critical to think through how they should be managed. A protected book list assures that children are not rereading a book in one grade after they read it in a previous grade. In our work in the schools, we would often see the popular books being read over and over in the upper grades. Establishing a school-protected book list requires collaboration among the teachers, resulting in capacity building for the literacy program within the school.

Questions of how to store so many books were raised in the planning stage of the library in the photo. It was suggested that plastic bins with lids might work as a possible solution. The main school librarian arranged the collection in bins for easy, organized access. Please see Appendix A for more information on setting up a novel sets library.

Where do you visualize a novel sets library in your school?

Professional Development Library

New balanced literacy schools have a well-stocked **professional development library** for teachers to have access to best practice materials. Nace (2013) believes that this type of professional development library can empower teachers to become independent learners. The collection now must include professional development to support CCSS instruction and assessment. The professional development library houses an array of current literature surrounding best practices in literacy and pedagogy. Access to information on the best and most current practices allows for ongoing professional development to continue. The literacy and grade-level teams can suggest books for the professional book clubs, encouraging participation and ongoing professional development. Videos can also be included in the library.

This display shows many current best practice books available. Please see Appendix A for more information on setting up a professional development library.

Where do you visualize a professional development library in your school?

The New Classroom Libraries

In new balanced literacy schools, classrooms are well stocked with books for children to read independently and for ongoing research. Most importantly, classroom libraries have at least 50 percent informational books from which to select. The range and variety of topics for appeal will be most important for the independent reading time. Teachers need to be sure that the books match both the interests and needs of the students while also offering challenge and complexity. We recommend that the classroom teacher do an informal reading interest assessment the first week of school in order to determine the range of interests within the classroom.

Another possibility is to send a letter home to parents asking them to identify the reading interests of their children before the start of the school year. The interests of the children will change, demanding that the library collections be updated often.

Classroom libraries have been an important component of best practices in literacy. However, teachers and administrators often struggle with instituting classroom libraries. Setting up a library can be a challenge for both new and veteran teachers. Some teachers inherit classroom libraries and are not sure where to go with them, while others begin in a barren classroom and have to start from the ground up. It is important to note here that, in general, teachers need support and guidance in setting up and maintaining a classroom library. Having teachers share their library ideas during grade-level meetings and even having teachers see each other's libraries is a good way to build capacity. Please see Appendix A for more information on setting up a classroom library.

The School Hallbrary

The idea that access to books has no limits is central to the notion of a hallbrary. The idea for the hallbrary evolved as principals discussed open spaces in schools where they envisioned bookshelves and places for reading aloud to small groups of children by teachers or volunteers. The concept is certainly interesting as the previously underutilized spaces in schools can be filled with books, sending the inherent message of their importance. In many of the schools, the children utilize the hallbraries when going to the lunchroom, waiting in the office, or walking down the hallways. The hallbrary sends a special, recurring message to students that books are both treasured and valued within the school.

These hallbraries can provide books for many purposes, including read-alouds for small groups, materials for one-on-one work, and enabling public access. Another function of hallbraries can be to highlight or feature new books to the school, holiday books, summer reading ideas, and more. In one school, the hallbrary is located on the second floor of a school. It is just off to the right at the top of the stairwell. Many children and teachers pass these books throughout the day. It is a perfect place to sit and read with a child during the day. Please see Appendix A for more information on setting up a hallbrary.

Where do you visualize a hallbrary in your school?

For all of the libraries, circulation is always a question that must be addressed even before the development of the library. A simple clipboard or notebook allows lenders to include their names and the date the books were checked out. This honor system is practiced effectively in many schools. See Appendix A for more information on access, circulation, and management of the individual libraries.

Organizational and Structural Changes: The Literacy Team, Grade-Level Teams, and Ongoing Professional Development

In balanced literacy schools, literacy teams and grade-level teams have regularly scheduled times to meet. These teams form the backbone and driving force of capacity building through collaboration. In moving to become a balanced literacy school, we recommend beginning with the formation of a literacy team and the development of grade-level teams. (See Chapter Four for more specific information on teams.)

> *In balanced literacy schools, professional development is ongoing and systematic.*

Ongoing and Systematic Professional Development

We believe rigorous, systematic, and ongoing professional development that includes a **collaborative, school-wide** effort on the CCSS is both critical and essential. The standards "do not tell teachers how to teach, but they do help teachers figure out the knowledge and skills their students should have so that teachers can build the best lessons and environments for their classrooms" (see "Frequently Asked Questions" on the CCSS website). The new balanced literacy model is an effective system to teach the requirements of CCSS and reading and writing within the content areas. Some of the main points emphasized in CCSS are precisely what balanced literacy emphasizes. Teachers need ongoing professional development to increase both their understanding of the changes mandated by the CCSS and their complement of skills in order to differentiate instruction so that all students have the opportunity to meet the standards.

Fisher and Frey (2012) discuss the need for teachers to be able to talk with their peers and develop their decision-making skills within professional learning communities. Our goal is to have teachers learn about their craft in an ongoing manner. This can happen in many ways within a school. First, teachers can attend professional development workshops that focus on a particular subject area. For example, we have provided workshops for schools over a three-year period that build upon the knowledge base of balanced literacy, capacity building, and CCSS. Grade-level and literacy team meetings can be a source of ongoing professional learning. Other opportunities during the school day can include peer observations and classroom walk-throughs. In one school, teachers did a walk-through of classrooms after school to share word walls with each other. Capacity building within a school positions teachers to be ongoing learners of their craft. Collaboration provides an opportunity to share practices with each other. We also see other times in schools when a teacher will ask us questions centering on their instruction or a particular student they are concerned about. This ongoing reflection about pedagogy and meeting students' needs is also part of teacher learning and development. (See Chapter Four for more information on professional development.)

Ways to Build in Ongoing and Systematic Professional Development

Professional development workshops	Develop a three-year plan of topics. (See Appendix E.)
Grade-level team meetings	Set an agenda and protocol that has built-in learning (analyzing student data, sharing teaching strategies).
Literacy team meetings	Hold book clubs, read short articles, attend conferences.
Transparent and shared practices	Use peer observations to share pedagogy and learning firsthand; conduct classroom walk-throughs to share classroom libraries, centers, word walls, and language walls.

What is your definition of the **new balanced literacy***?*

Where do you think your school is at with implementing the Common Core State Standards?

Where do you think your school is at with the new balanced literacy model?

Chapter Two: Instructional Tenets

The Influence of Common Core on Balanced Literacy

Guiding Questions:

- What are the tenets of the new balanced literacy?
- What are the instructional shifts necessary for CCSS?

Schools that identify themselves as balanced literacy driven often focus on key curriculum components. These components are delivered daily in reading and writing workshops. Teachers typically utilize the instructional methods listed below in balanced literacy classrooms.

Typical Instruction in a Balanced Literacy Classroom

- Read-Alouds and Shared Reading
- Guided Reading
- Literacy Centers
- Independent Reading
- Book Club
- Word Walls
- Classroom Libraries
- Independent Writing

Changing Instruction to Meet Common Core Demands

The CCSS mission statement takes the position that the standards are to "provide a consistent, clear understanding of what students are expected to learn, so teachers and parents know what they need to do to help them. The standards are designed to be robust and relevant to the real world" (CCSS website). This is indeed both a grand and robust mission for states to adhere to and for schools to institute in a successful manner. The new balanced literacy model is an effective system to teach CCSS along with reading and writing within the content areas.

There has been widespread agreement about the shifts of instruction necessary for student success and implementation of the CCSS. Three shifts have had a major influence on the re-conceptualized model of balanced literacy; thus, the new balanced literacy model emerged from these six instructional shifts. The development of the CCSS ELA and math standards grew out of a partnership between Achieve, the National Governors Association (NGA), and the Council of Chief State School Officers (CCSSO). Achieve is also supporting the states with the implementation of the standards (Achieve, 2012). The three instructional shifts as outlined by Achieve follow.

Three Instructional Shifts Necessary for Success with Common Core in ELA/Literacy

3 Common Core Shifts for English Language Arts/Literacy

Regular practice with complex text and its academic language

Rather than focusing solely on the skills of reading and writing, the Standards highlight the growing complexity of the texts students must read to be ready for the demands of college and careers. The Standards build a staircase of text complexity so that all students are ready for the demands of college- and career-level reading no later than the end of high school. Closely related to text complexity—and inextricably connected to reading comprehension—is a focus on academic vocabulary: words that appear in a variety of content areas (such as ignite and commit).

Reading, writing and speaking grounded in evidence from text, both literary and informational

The Standards place a premium on students writing to sources, i.e., using evidence from texts to present careful analyses, well-defended claims, and clear information. Rather than asking students questions they can answer solely from their prior knowledge or experience, the Standards expect students to answer questions that depend on their having read the text or texts with care. The standards also require the cultivation of narrative writing throughout the grades, and in later grades a command of sequence and detail will be essential for effective argumentative and informational writing. Likewise, the reading standards focus on students' ability to read carefully and grasp information, arguments, ideas, and details based on text evidence. Students should be able to answer a range of text-dependent questions, questions in which the answers require inferences based on careful attention to the text.

Building knowledge through content-rich nonfiction

Building knowledge through content rich nonfiction plays an essential role in literacy and in the Standards. In K–5, fulfilling the standards requires a 50–50 balance between informational and literary reading. Informational reading primarily includes content-rich nonfiction in history/social studies, science, and the arts; the K–5 Standards strongly recommend that students build coherent general knowledge both within each year and across years. In 6–12, ELA classes place much greater attention to a specific category of informational text—literary nonfiction—than has been traditional. In grades 6–12, the Standards for literacy in history/social studies, science and technical subjects ensure that students can independently build knowledge in these disciplines through reading and writing.

To be clear, the Standards do require substantial attention to literature throughout K–12, as half of the required work in K–5 and the core of the work of 6–12 ELA teachers.

These three instructional shifts have been identified by Achieve and have informed our work in re-conceptualizing balanced literacy. We have taken these shifts and integrated them in all the tenets of balanced literacy. No doubt, there is certainly a sense of urgency to bring about these shifts into the classroom. However, most schools will need capacity building in order to do so. Also important here is a recognition that these changes will take time to implement and may take years to fully realize. The deliberate decisions about these instructional shifts will take extensive professional development time as well.

Shanahan (2013) identifies eight challenging shifts in instruction with respect to the CCSS that overlap with the Achieve three. The use of challenging texts, for example, will bring about some discomfort and struggle for both teachers and children. Close reading of challenging and informational texts is viewed as another challenge as children will need to be guided through the grades on this topic. Close reading, according to CCSS Anchor Standard 1, means to "Read closely to determine what the text says explicitly and to make logical inferences from it; cite specific textual evidence when writing or speaking to support conclusions drawn from the text." Teachers will need to thoroughly understand close reading and strategies for its application in the classroom. Another shift, disciplinary literacy, requires attention to a new kind of reading text. Teachers and reading specialists have not been trained in reading in the disciplines, especially in the upper grades that the standards require. Reading in science, history, social studies, and other subjects now takes new skills and strategies to execute. While past standards emphasized reading a single text, 15 percent of all the ELA standards now require reading and interpreting multiple texts (a fifth challenging shift) throughout all the grades, covering reading, writing, and speaking. Writing to build an argument and citing evidence will be two more major shifts in instruction for all grades and content areas. And finally, the need to include 21st century research and communication tools will demand a shift in thinking about how to use digital tools and technology for all reading, writing, and communication.

Shanahan's Eight Big Challenging Shifts for CCSS

Shanahan's (2013) eight big shifts in instruction with respect to the CCSS include:

- Challenging text
- Close reading
- Informational text
- Multiple texts
- Disciplinary literacy (grades six through 12)
- Argument
- 21st century research and communication tools
- Writing about sources

The photo to the right is a collection of all the exemplar texts from Appendix B of the Common Core State Standards. This school had the entire set housed in a special area of their balanced literacy room.

Sample Common Core Standard on Informational Texts

The following standard is an example that indicates the shift in focus to complex and informational texts.

CCSS.ELA-Literacy.CCRA.R.10: Read and comprehend complex literary and informational texts independently and proficiently.

Aligning the Three Instructional Shifts to the Tenets of Balanced Literacy

The new framework for balanced literacy has been influenced by the three instructional shifts that are described by Achieve and the eight big shifts described by Shanahan. We took each of the shifts and changes necessary for success with CCSS and then aligned them with the tenets of balanced literacy. The following shows how each of the tenets has been redefined by the instructional shifts.

Tenets of Balanced Literacy	CCSS Shifts in Instructional Strategies
New read-aloud	The new read-aloud reflects the language of learners. Fifty percent of the texts used in kindergarten through fifth grade are exemplar informational and complex texts, and the percent increases to 70 for grades six through 12. The read-alouds include all content areas and poetry while modeling close reading, repeated readings, and written responses. Teachers make intertextual connections, use academic vocabulary within the social discourse, and have rigorous conversations. Language is in action during read-alouds.
New guided reading into language	The new guided reading/writing includes guiding language into literacy as a staircase of complexity and using language to guide, scaffold, and inform all literacy instruction, including phonemic awareness through comprehension, close readings, and repeated readings, with 50 percent informational and complex text. Teachers guide students into developing text-based answers and habits of evidentiary arguments through social discourse and academic vocabulary. Book club serves as a way to guide language into reading, especially in the intermediate and upper grades. Students are guided through 21st century research/communication tools.

Tenets of Balanced Literacy	CCSS Shifts in Instructional Strategies
Language and literacy centers	Center projects can include solving problems, reading with a partner, raising issues, writing research reports, generating discussions, preparing research presentations, and building arguments and persuasion individually and in teams. These projects revolve around using 21st century research and communication tools.
Word walls to language walls	Word walls become language walls, building vocabulary for social discourse and academic knowledge as well as comprehension and communication, all generating new understandings.
New Independent reading	A balance of informational and disciplinary literacy texts (science, social studies, etc.) helps students access the world of knowledge, read complex texts to find evidence and build knowledge, and read for different purposes.
New independent writing	There is a focus on knowledge of language and language conventions for opinion and persuasion, generative, informative and explanatory, and narrative writing. Students participate in shared and peer research and writing, and writing from text sources. Evidence to inform or make an argument is practiced as is compare and contrast. Students increase the time spent writing, increase the motivation for writing, use technology, and write responses from discourse while implementing 21st century research and communication tools.
New classroom libraries	Classroom libraries have exemplar texts on such text types as informational, complex, and poetry, as well as an array of genres that meet all of the necessary text types, including disciplinary texts.

What Does Common Core Look Like in a New Balanced Literacy Classroom?

The New Read-Aloud

Guiding Questions:

- Why do we read stories aloud to children?
- How do I plan for a new read-aloud in my classroom?
- How much time is devoted to reading aloud?
- What are some read-aloud titles that align with CCSS?
- How can we encourage parents to read aloud at home?
- How about reading aloud in all the disciplines?

One of the goals of a new balanced literacy school is to have a read-aloud every day in every classroom. This includes all content-area teachers as well as art, music, technology, and physical education teachers. We believe all teachers should be reading aloud daily to children. Daily read-alouds are a signature characteristic of balanced literacy classrooms. Decisions about what selection to read aloud, along with skills and strategies to teach and reinforce, are part of the ongoing efforts that contribute to best practices in literacy. In the new read-aloud, children have the opportunity to listen to informational text at least 50 percent of the read-aloud time. Teachers balance narrative and informational text while children are engaged in finding text-based answers and close reading during rigorous conversations. In the photo above, the teacher was reading an informational book by Steven Jenkins and asking the children prediction questions as he read aloud. The children (who are not pictured) are responding to the read-aloud questions using whiteboards, making it an interactive read-aloud with informational text.

What makes the new read-aloud different and distinctive is that the teacher is making different decisions surrounding the selection, questions, and overall instruction. The new read-aloud is longer as the focus of the lesson is different from the past. The teacher stops more often to instruct, model close reading, and engage the children in serious conversations that invoke discourse. From this discourse, children have the opportunity to learn about developing arguments from the evidence in the selection that the teacher has read. The teacher may pause during the read-aloud to model a close reading behavior, which will draw the children's attention to certain aspects of the text and to specific details and information.

Close reading is defined as an instructional routine in which students critically examine a text, especially through repeated readings (Fisher and Frey, 2012). During close reading, teachers ask questions that require students to find evidence from the text to determine their responses rather than solely from their prior knowledge of the subject. Responses to questions are text-based driven and require text-based answers. Fisher and Frey (2012) further outline two primary purposes of close reading:

- "To afford with students the opportunity to assimilate new textual information with their existing background knowledge and prior experiences to expand their schema
- To build the necessary habits of readers when they engage with a complex piece of text"

While children are not actually engaged in the act of close reading during the read-aloud, the teacher is modeling the behaviors and showing what the children will learn to do when reading on their own. For example, the teacher might underline key ideas, use sticky notes to record notes, post a question, or jot down an important word in the text. Rereading or repeated reading of a read-aloud is commonly seen with bedtime stories as children will frequently request a story they have heard before. Thus, the concept of rereading a story over and over again is not new to children as many of them are used to stories being reread to them at home. What is new is taking this practice into the classroom and reading a selection aloud a second or third time to children. When repeating a read-aloud, teachers need to go deeper into the text the second time around, knowing that background knowledge has already been established. For more information on close reading and how to develop close reading accounts for children, please see Appendix F.

Reading aloud an informational text requires a different delivery than reading a narrative story, and children react differently to each of these text types. Both reader responses are important, but the differences need to be noted as an important aspect of the new read-aloud. Daily read-alouds are not just for the classroom teacher but for all teachers, including art, physical education, music, and technology. In art, teachers can read fiction, nonfiction, biographies, and informational books about art and artists. A read-aloud can be connected to classroom research, art lessons, and writing. In music, teachers can read aloud books about music and biographies of musicians, and students can research topics while learning and practicing the skills in the classroom. In the physical education class, the teacher can read aloud selections on sports, exercise, wellness, nutrition, and the human body. Teachers can read stories of triumph and sports heroes and much more. In technology class, we saw one teacher read aloud a story about a character who plagiarized an assignment—a great selection with an embedded lesson about consequences. Successful read-alouds take place in math classes as well. Appendix B of CCSS has a list of exemplar texts for all subjects discussed here.

The New Read-Aloud Teacher Classroom Inventory

As you begin to think about scheduled daily read-alouds, take a few moments to self-reflect on these questions surrounding your own practices. The purpose of this inventory is to bring your own read-aloud practices to the center stage. Use this as a starting point to deeply develop your own ideas and practices regarding daily read-aloud.

The New Read-Aloud Teacher Classroom Inventory

1. About how often do you read aloud to your class?
2. How often do you read informational and nonfiction selections to your class?
3. About how long do you spend reading a selection to your class?
4. Do you ever reread the selection as a repeated reading to your class?
5. How do you decide what selection to read to your class?
6. Do you model close reading behaviors with your students?
7. Do you consider the text complexity when you decide on a selection?
8. Does your school have a read-aloud library?
9. Do you share and collaborate about your read-aloud with your peers?
10. Is there time in grade-level team meetings to collaborate and share about read-aloud?
11. Do you think about pairing up a fictional passage with a nonfiction or an informational text?
12. What kinds of questions do you ask when you read aloud?
13. How do students interact when you read aloud?
14. Do you allow time for rich conversations to evolve from the read-aloud?
15. Do you give students a chance to find evidence in the text from your read-aloud?

What's New? at-a-Glance: The New Read-Aloud

- 50 percent informational and challenging text in kindergarten through fifth grade
- 70 percent informational and challenging text in grades six and up
- Teacher models close reading
- Teacher asks text-based questions
- Repeated reading is emphasized
- All content areas and poetry are covered
- Social discourse is generated throughout
- Rich conversations and academic vocabulary are used
- Read-alouds take place in all the content areas, including art, music, physical education, and technology

Teacher Tips for the New Read-Aloud in All Grades

- Aim for at least two daily read-alouds, and pair up a fictional passage with a nonfiction or informational text.
- Connect or tie in the two read-alouds to a common theme. For example, if you are studying the ocean, you could read any informational book and connect it to a fiction book that involves the ocean.
- Read poetry selections from the Common Core exemplars, which may be found in Appendix B of CCSS, or other favorite poems, and model close reading.
- Take your time during read-alouds; consider rereading a selection, and model close reading behaviors.
- Think about text complexity when deciding upon a book; take the students to a more challenging level when possible.
- Make your read-alouds interactive. Have students use small whiteboards to respond to questions you pose. Younger children can draw their response and older children can write out responses.
- Ask higher-level questions as you read to align with the standards. (Do you agree or disagree and why? Show evidence for your answer.)
- Promote social discourse during your read-aloud, and always give time for serious and humorous conversations about the information you are reading.
- Go from a word wall to a language wall from the rich conversations and discourse that evolve from the read-aloud.

- Keep track of the read-alouds you have completed, and post them publicly for the children and school community to see, such as outside your classroom. Share this list periodically with parents to show the amount of books and subjects covered.
- Celebrate your read-aloud selections by placing them in a prominent place in the classroom. Cookbook stands work well for all books, and clear plastic napkin holders display chapter books well.

Teacher Tips for the New Read-Aloud in Grades Five through Eight

- 70 percent of the read-alouds should be informational and complex texts in grades six and above.
- Be ambitious and bold in selecting informational texts for older students.
- Make reading aloud an important part of your daily routine.
- Select challenging texts to read aloud and stretch students' thinking during the lesson.
- Select chapter books that are engaging and will be sure to capture students' interests.
- Model close reading during read-aloud, and repeat the reading when appropriate.

The tips on the following page can be made into a one-sheet handout or bookmark for the parent library (see Appendix A).

Six Tips for Reading Aloud

1. **Love it:** Love the selection you are reading.
2. **Practice it:** Read the selection silently and aloud more than once.
3. **Stretch it:** Open the book wide and stretch it for all in the audience to see pictures, etc.
4. **Express it:** Use expression as you read.
5. **Post it:** Post notes on the back.
6. **Question it:** What do you think will happen next?

Love the Book

- Read books that you enjoy reading.
- Read books that capture your enthusiasm.
- Read books that you love to hear and see.
- Read books that have won awards.
- Read books that make you feel good.
- Read books by authors you love.

Practice Reading the Book

- Read the book silently to yourself.
- Read the book aloud.
- Read to find interesting words.
- Read to find beautiful and interesting illustrations.
- Read the book to see how long it takes.

Stretch the Book

- Stretch the book wide open when you read.
- Stretch your arms out so all can see pictures.
- Stretch left to right and up and down to the audience.
- Think about the logistics of where you are in relation to your audience.
- Think about how the book stretches the audience: Are the children on the floor, at desks, or at tables?

Express the Book

- Whisper if you hear a soft message.
- Raise your voice for a loud thought.
- Read as if you are the character.
- Be as animated as possible.
- Use vocal and facial expressions.
- Exaggerate your words when appropriate.

Post Ideas Before Reading

- Use sticky notes on the back of the book as reminders.
- Identify the title, author, illustrator, and special features.
- Post a page and highlight a word.
- Post expression reminders.
- Post a question: What do you think will happen next?

Question It: Directed Reading Thinking Activity (DRTA)

- Look at the title, and look at the picture.
- What do you think the story is going to be about?
- Stop at key points and ask, "What do you think will happen next?"

An excellent way to display your read-aloud selection is to stand it up on a plastic cookbook stand.

New Read-Aloud and the Home-School Connection

Parent libraries that are well stocked with bedtime stories naturally encourage parents to read at home to their children. When parents have access to books, it makes it that much easier to read year round. One of the most important gifts a parent can give a child is the nightly bedtime story. These special moments will add up to cherished memories that are treasured for life. The bedtime story that evolves into a nightly routine can nurture and support the love and enjoyment of books, stories, and reading (Policastro, 2008). Further, reading aloud to children can provide an array of important and critical experiences in supporting the development of evolving and emergent literacy. The bedtime story can be a family affair providing a special time to sit close, relax, and get closure on the day. In essence, this routine can be the centerpiece of the evening. Fisher and Medvic (2000) describe the bedtime story as a positive experience where parent and child enjoy themselves together. They add that the bedtime story can be a humorous, playful, relaxed, respectful, and cozy experience. In the new read-aloud, parents are encouraged to move into informational texts as an important source for home reading.

Establishing the Bedtime Story Routine: Tips for Parents

Encouraging parents to read every night is an important goal in establishing strong home-school partnerships. Just imagine if parents read every night to their children: That would be 365 stories! Here are a few tips for helping parents establish a nightly routine. We suggest having these tips available in the parent library collection (see Appendix A):

- Start with favorites to return to. It is perfectly fine to reread a book. Children love repeated readings and never tire of favorites like *Goodnight Moon* by Margaret Wise Brown.
- Encourage parents to read aloud informational texts half of the time.
- Read every night. Establish a routine by reading near the same time each evening. Always turn off the TV and limit other distractions.
- Ask simple questions as you read, such as, "What do you think will happen next in the story?"
- Keep books near the bed; establish a bedtime story shelf or nook.

Recommended Informational Texts for Read-Aloud

Adamson, T. K. (2012). *Basketball: The math of the game.* Sports math. North Mankato, MN: Capstone.

Allen, K. (2010). *The science of a rock concert: Sound in action.* North Mankato, MN: Capstone.

Barr, L. (2004). *Volcano! When a mountain explodes.* North Mankato, MN: Capstone.

Burgan, M. (2014). *Ellis Island: An interactive history adventure.* North Mankato, MN: Capstone.

Dell, P., Raatma, L., & Tougas, S. (2012). *Science of war* series. North Mankato, MN: Capstone.

Easterling, L. (2008). *Music.* North Mankato, MN: Capstone.

Freedman, R. (1989). *Lincoln: A photobiography.* New York, NY: Clarion Books.

Guillain, C. (2009). *Space* series. North Mankato, MN: Capstone.

Gunderson, J. (2007). *The last rider: The final days of the Pony Express.* North Mankato, MN: Capstone.

Hunt, J. (2014). *Greek myths and legends.* North Mankato, MN: Capstone.

Lassieur, A. (2014). *The Harlem renaissance: An interactive history adventure.* North Mankato, MN: Capstone.

Llewellyn, C. (2013). *Oceans.* North Mankato, MN: Capstone.

MacKay, D.A. (2010). *The building of Manhattan.* Illustrated by: Donald A. MacKay. Mineola, NY: Dover Publishing, Inc.

Mark, J. (2007). *The museum book: A guide to strange and wonderful collections.* Illustrated by: Richard Holland. Somerville, MA: Candlewick.

Markel, M. (2013). *Brave Girl: Clara and the Shirtwaist Strike of 1909.* Illustrated by: Melissa Sweet. New York, NY: Balzer & Bray.

Moss, L. (2000). *Zin! Zin! Zin! A violin.* Illustrated by: Marjorie Priceman. New York, NY: Aladdin Picture Books.

Murphy, J. (2010). *The great fire.* New York, NY: Scholastic Paperbacks.

Pappas, T. (1997). *The adventures of Penrose the mathematical cat.* San Carlos, CA: Wide World Publishing.

Partridge, E. (2002). *This land was made for you and me.* New York, NY: Viking Juvenile.

Peterson, I., & Henderson, N. (1999). *Math trek: Adventures in the MathZone.* San Francisco, CA: Jossey-Bass.

Pfeffer, W. (2004). *From seed to pumpkin.* Illustrated by: James Graham Hale. New York, NY: HarperCollins.

Ruffin, F. E. (2000). *Martin Luther King, Jr. and the march on Washington.* Illustrated by: Stephen Marchesi. New York, NY: Penguin Young Readers.

O'Donnell, L. (2007). *Blackbeard's sword: The pirate king of the Carolinas.* North Mankato, MN: Capstone.

Ramsey, C.A. (2010). *Ruth and the green book.* Illustrated by: Floyd Cooper. Minneapolis, MN: Carolrhoda Books.

Ruurs, M. (2005). *My librarian is a camel: How books are brought to children around the world.* Honesdale, PA: Boyds Mills Press.

Sateren, S. (2003). *Monet.* North Mankato, MN: Capstone.

Smith, D. J. (2011). *If the world were a village.* Illustrated by: Shelagh Armstrong. Tonawanda, NY: Kids Can Press.

St. George, J. (2004). *So you want to be president?* Illustrated by: David Small. New York, NY: Philomel.

Tang, G. (2004). *The grapes of math.* Illustrated by: Harry Briggs. New York, NY: Scholastic Paperbacks.

Tougas, S. (2012). *Little Rock girl 1957: How a photograph changed the fight for integration.* North Mankato, MN: Capstone.

Waldron, M., Llewellyn, C., & Silverman, B. (2013). *Habitat Survival* series. North Mankato, MN: Capstone.

The New Guided Reading: Guiding Language into Reading

Guiding Questions:

- What is the definition of the *new guided reading*?
- What influence does language have on instruction?
- Where does book club belong in a new balanced literacy classroom?

The new guided reading into language routine showing argument

Guided reading continues to be considered a best practice in general education and is used in thousands of classrooms around the world (Ferguson and Wilson, 2009; Fountas and Pinnell, 2012). There is no question that there are many connections to guided reading and the CCSS. However, Shanahan (2013) points out that the placement of students in leveled books, according to Fountas and Pinnell, means placing them in books they can read with better than 90 percent accuracy and high comprehension. CCSS requires that students in grade two and above read more challenging texts during instruction (IRA, 2012), and this means placing students in more challenging texts. This shift will require a different kind of thinking and instruction. Teachers will need to provide more time for students to read and the appropriate scaffolding for students to understand these more challenging texts. Fountas and Pinnell (2012) believe that not only should students be reading books independently to build interest, stamina, and fluency, but they should also be able to tackle harder books to provide the opportunity to grow as a more skillful reader. They contend that this processing of more challenging texts is made possible by an expert teacher's careful text selection and strong teaching and recognize that this important teacher knowledge takes time to develop.

During our summer reading clinic, we have the opportunity to match challenging texts to readers. In one instance, a student was interested in mud wrestling and we had a difficult time finding anything appropriate. The local library bookmobile was on campus for its weekly visit to the clinic when the librarian heard the student requesting books on the topic of mud wrestling. Sure enough, the next week, the librarian returned with books about mud wrestling. These books were complex and challenging for the reader. However, he dove into the text with voracious energy. Another student who was identified as a struggling, low-level reader appeared one day with challenging reading materials about the field of podiatry. He was quite interested in the information and learning everything he could as his father was studying to become a podiatrist. Often, children will surprise us with the level of challenging and complex texts that they are both willing and happy to interact with. In many cases, when the interest of the student is matched, the complexity of the text becomes secondary. This is especially important now as we seek ways to find challenging text for students in grades two through eight that are above their instructional and independent reading levels.

Characteristics of Guided Reading (Fountas and Pinnell, 1996, 2012)

- Guided reading is situated in a strong balanced literacy program.
- Guided reading is just one component of balanced literacy.
- A child participates in small-group instruction that is organized, structured, and planned for 10 to 30 minutes a day.
- Children are placed in groups based on similar reading behaviors.
- The teacher provides interactive read-alouds with the whole class (not leveled books).
- Students participate in whole-group, small-group, and individual instruction, as well as reading and writing workshops, shared writing, and writing aloud.
- Children participate in guided thought.
- Word study is taught through phonics and spelling.
- There is a purpose to the whole process, where children are guided and supported by the teacher through the reading lesson.
- Guided reading matches books to readers. The teacher selects a text that will be just right to support student learning. Matching books to readers means finding texts that require readers to work out problems or learn new strategies.

What Do Good Readers Do? (Fountas and Pinnell, 1996, 1999, and 2012)

- Good readers focus on meaning while reading.
- Good readers use their knowledge of language as a source of information while reading.
- Good readers have a wide range of strategies for solving words.
- Good readers process print with fluency and phrasing.
- Good readers go beyond the text to interpret, summarize, synthesize, and evaluate information.

New Guided Language into Reading and Writing

Guiding Questions:

- How do I group students for small-group instruction?
- How do I select text that reflects a gradient of text complexity?
- How do I use language to guide instruction with small groups of students?
- How is close reading different from repeated reading?

Another goal of a new balanced literacy school is to have small-group instruction every day. Teachers should consider these elements:

- Physical environment
- Grouping of students
- Text selection
- Type of reading during small-group time
- Discourse during the guided reading
- Vocabulary instruction

Grouping Students for Small-Group Instruction and Selecting Complex Text

A guided reading table for all grades and small-group instruction

Physical space is so critical for small-group instruction. Over the years, we have come to realize that a kidney-shaped table is essential for small-group instruction, whether it is in a kindergarten classroom or an eighth-grade classroom. This specialized table says to the students that small-group instruction is important. In addition, it says that small-group instruction is part of our everyday classroom routine. A physical space also helps designate and restrict group size.

Time for small-group instruction is another key element. It is more important to have frequency than length. We have developed a routine (explained in detail in Chapter Three) that we call 110 Minutes of Daily Balanced Literacy. This routine provides time for small-group instruction every day and not randomly. The teacher needs to observe on a daily basis how students are reading, thinking, and comprehending text. This daily interaction allows the teacher to collect data either through running records or anecdotal notes in order to make adjustments in text selection or grouping. Without this routine, the systematic data collection is missed and smooth, and effective scaffolding of instruction does not occur.

Grouping is one of the easiest and hardest elements for teachers to think through. While many teachers have used running records to group students for guided reading according to similar levels of text, in a new balanced literacy model, new criteria for grouping is needed. New means of grouping can be based on text complexities and include:

1. The qualitative aspects or purposes for reading.
2. The reader and the task or motivation and experience the student brings to the text.
3. The quantitative aspects, such as the style and format the author used while writing the text.

A student may not know about wizards or Muggles but is nonetheless motivated to read the *Harry Potter* books by J. K. Rowling. The student's purpose in reading the books might not be to learn about wizards or the theme of loyalty and friendship, but to be part of a peer group that is also reading and discussing the books. A student who loves the University of Notre Dame Fighting Irish football team will be inspired to read about the best or most famous coach because he personally wants to know about this person. This rethinking of grouping based on purpose and student motivation, along with text complexity—especially with nonfiction—is new and different.

Another way of thinking about grouping and text complexity is through the use of unit instruction. Teachers who use units that are based on themes and begin with important questions students want to discuss—instead of superficial questions—can guide instruction that is more complex and use language to support learning. Significant questions that do not have obvious answers can create opportunities for social discourse. For example, a group of students reading about cats and dogs can discover which animal makes a better pet. The students first read informational texts during the guided reading session and then have to present an argument about why their pet was a better choice. In this case, the students are reading for a clear purpose and need to be able to support their answers based on what the text or evidence states, not their own opinion or prior knowledge. In a group we observed, discussion that occurred after the reading was intense and the students not only defined and defended their positions, but continued the conversation after the small-group instruction ended. The arguments presented were persuasive and caused a couple of children to rethink their selection of pets. This is the goal of new guided reading: to have language as the vehicle that guides students into thinking differently about what and how they read.

Previously, teachers would have based their grouping on text levels. As indicated in the above scenario, groupings were instead based on interest and, more importantly, on informational text that enabled students to use facts and not opinions to present their case, which was guided by the essential question. Opitz and Ford (2001) discuss taking the reader, context, and text into account and going beyond simply matching a reader to a reading level. The types of decisions a teacher makes to create these opportunities are different from the traditional decisions based on text levels. This type of scaffolding calls for the teacher to begin with higher-order questions and then map backward to the type of text and complexity needed to answer the question or questions. Teachers also must consider whether that text enables students to use the information gleaned from it.

In the CCSS model of text complexity, the terms that are used for choosing text are qualitative evaluation, quantitative evaluation, and matching the reader to the text and task. These elements are meant to be considered together, providing the most opportunities for students to discuss and think deeply about the text.

In order to have these rich conversations, students need to learn how to do close reading. One of the simplest ways to achieve close reading is to engage in multiple readings of the text. Each rereading of a text can have a different purpose. The first reading might be to get a literal understanding of the passage; the second might be for specific information; and the third might be for the nuances of the vocabulary, author's style, presentation, or purposes. Thus, each reading has students think about the text in a different way. Additionally, these rereadings enable students to learn not only from the text but about the text as well.

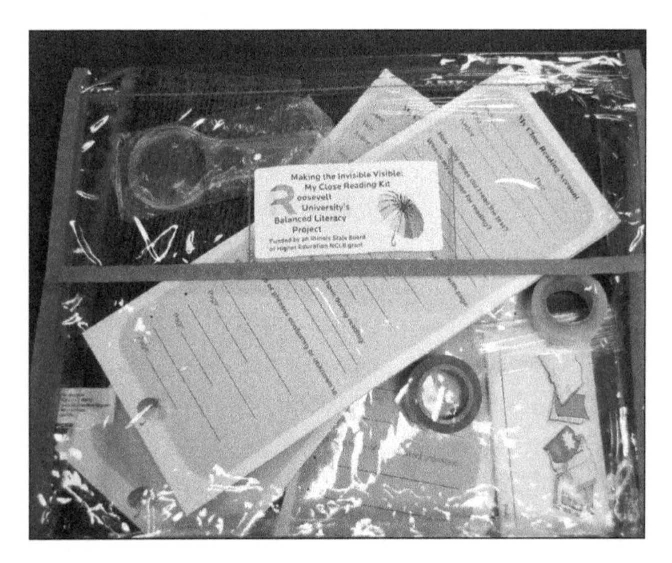

In most of the schools we work with, children do not have the opportunity to write in their books for close reading. Consequently, we developed the My Close Reading Account, where students can use the account sheet like a bookmark as they read. (See picture.) We wanted a way for students to document their close reading activities in an authentic manner—and not like a workbook page. See Appendix F for reading account sheets for primary, intermediate, and upper grades.

Book Club as a Way to Guide Language into Reading

The ultimate goal for guiding language into reading and writing is to create new habits of thinking that are supported by evidence and not by personal opinion. We want children to be thoughtful with their answers, persistent in pursuing those answers, flexible in their thinking, and able to listen and apply knowledge for constructive means. Books club is a great way to accomplish these goals.

Guiding Questions:

- Where can book club get started?
- How can informational and challenging texts be used in book club?
- How can book club be used in all the grades?

Book Club in the New Balanced Literacy Classroom

We have been advocates of book club for many years as it has served us well in the preparation of both pre-service and in-service teachers. We have learned that teachers seem perfectly comfortable using a book club approach for their own learning about literature and adapt well to the reader response theories. Thus, we have modeled book club as a serious, authentic way for teachers to think about teaching reading in their own classrooms in all grades. Most recently, we have found book club to be a perfect model to implement the CCSS.

Book club is an essential component of the balanced literacy school that plays out in many different forms. For example, it works well in the upper grades as a way to work in both large and small groups covering a novel. Book club can begin in the primary grades but works best in the upper grades as it guides student language into reading. Teachers can use book club to generate opportunities for classroom discourse while covering all of the CCSS instructional shifts, allowing for close reading, finding evidence, and developing arguments.

Guided reading is often a difficult practice for upper-grade teachers to implement. This challenge happens for many reasons. First, often in the upper grades, children change classes and are not in the same group throughout the school day. Teachers routinely talk about the difficulty of grouping students for a 50-minute block of time. Second, upper grades are often content-area driven and each teacher is responsible for teaching a content area like math, science, and social studies. Content-area teachers often view guided reading as a practice that takes place in the primary classroom only. Also, upper-grade classrooms are sometimes not set up for the small-group instruction needed for guided reading groups. We suggest that upper-grade teachers have the bean tables to facilitate and manage small-group instruction. However, book club can serve in much the same capacity as guided reading for older students, particularly in grades three through eight.

Book Club: What You Should Know

- Book club is defined as people meeting to discuss a book they have read and express opinions, likes, and dislikes.
- Book club emerged from the literature-based movements of the 1980s and early 1990s.
- Book club integrates reading, writing, listening, speaking, and viewing in authentic ways that make sense to children, teachers, and parents.
- Book club provides endless expansion possibilities.
- Book club promotes authentic conversation, discussion, and risk-taking.
- Book club is dialogic in nature (not monologic), as the students and teacher search for meaning and conversation that is collective and dynamic.

Teacher Tips for Book Club Implementation

- Book club is well suited for the balanced literacy classroom daily routines.
- Book club is perfect for guiding language into reading with classroom discourse with students.
- Book club engages students in rich and rigorous conversations.
- Book club can easily be integrated as part of the classroom reading and writing workshops.
- Book club works quite well in grades three through eight.
- Book club can certainly be adapted in kindergarten through third grade to meet the needs of younger children.
- Book club methods can be used in a guided reading group, especially in the upper grades.
- Book club can be 90 minutes a day for older children and 45 minutes a day for younger children.

The New Word Walls to Language Walls

Guiding Questions:

- What is a language wall?
- How does a language wall differ from a word wall?
- How does a language wall support students' discourse?

Balanced literacy classrooms are rich in print; words abound in many ways. For example, word walls provide an opportunity to systematically organize words within the classroom environment and can be displayed on any wall using large enough letters for the children to see from any seat in the classroom. In the new balanced literacy classroom, word walls transition to language walls. This is a natural progression with the focus now being centered on language and discourse. To help rich conversations evolve and expand from single words to larger discourse, the teacher can pause during guided reading time and specifically highlight the discussion with the language wall.

A student-created language wall for a parade

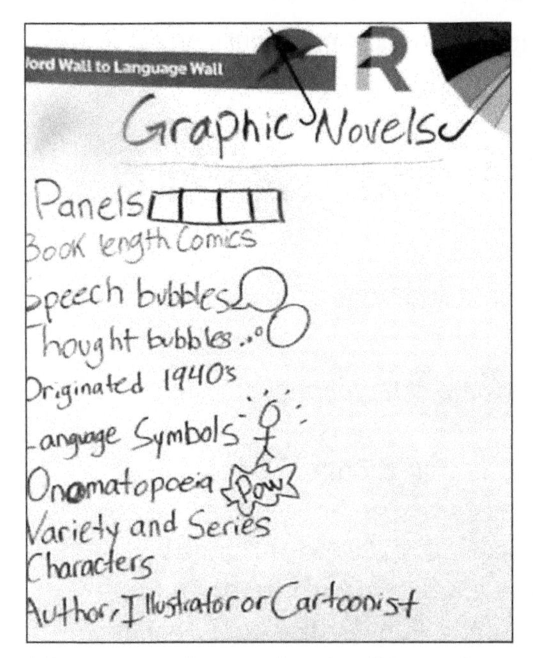

A language wall created on graphic novels

Language walls are word walls expanded to a more sophisticated level to include ideas, notions, images, and much more, providing for deeper discussions. Language walls foster both social and academic discourse, allowing the teacher to document specific aspects of language. In the example at left, the topic was graphic novels and the students discussed what defines or captures the essence of a graphic novel. This example moves beyond words to include the images and characteristics that define "graphic" within novels.

Language walls are ongoing within classrooms and evolve daily. Dry-erase boards work well and allow for a tremendous amount of language to transpire during the day. We have found that teachers who transition from word walls to language walls have added flexibility in teaching a lesson. The language evolves within the lesson, changing into the next discourse study. Language walls are now seen in PE, art, music, and math classes.

What's New? at-a-Glance: The New Word Wall to Language Wall

- Language walls allow for building vocabulary and language through social discourse.
- Language walls happen in all content areas, including art, math, music, physical education, and technology.
- The focus of a language wall is on language generation by the students.
- Language walls create new information and understanding about the world.
- Language walls promote rich conversations that foster comprehension and communication among students.

Teacher Tips for Using Word Walls to Language Walls for All Grades

- Stop and pause often when teaching and engage in rich conversations that evoke social discourse.
- Write down key ideas and elements of the subject matter being discussed.
- Capture the discourse through words, images, photographs, and other means to communicate the ideas, concepts, and beliefs about the lesson being taught.
- Keep the word wall to language wall visible so all children can see it.
- Continuously develop new language walls as part of instruction, discussion, and conversation.

Teacher Tips for Using Word Walls to Language Walls in Grades Five through Eight

- Create categories for words, such as academic words and non-academic words.
- Organize or associate words with a story or text.
- Create games and procedures for language walls to become interactive.

The big takeaway we want teachers to understand is that thoughtful speech can change how students think. Johnston (2004) showed how specific words, phrases, and even silence influenced classrooms. We are advocating that serious-minded discussions about more complex text for both fiction and nonfiction will have an impact on classroom instruction. We are also promoting discussion or discourse that is more precise and needs to be occurring in multiple routines in the classroom like the new read-alouds, guiding language into reading, language and literacy centers, and language walls.

What Does School and Classroom Discourse Look Like and Sound Like?

A classroom that has an emphasis on discourse focuses on the thoughtful decisions teachers make in setting up and creating the physical environment. Nooks and spaces are designed to invite students into conversations and for individual work. These spaces are attractive and have books and comfortable seating like the parent libraries and the hallbraries in schools. The classroom has the gentle murmur of conversations within small groups, conversations started by rigorous, higher-order questions so that children have opportunities to explore answers not only with text but with peers through deep and meaningful discussions.

Regular classroom discourse can build social and personal communication skills, but discourse that is started with more complex text and supported with higher-order questions will produce better conversations. The key to accomplishing this goal is planning. Teachers will need to:

- Identify the purpose of reading lessons.
- Create engaging spaces that promote talk and discussion.
- Manage the different areas and spaces.
- Create language and literacy centers that invite conversations.

The New Language and Literacy Centers

Guiding Questions:

- What is a center and how does it function in my classroom?
- How do you get started with the new language and literacy centers?
- How do you manage language and literacy centers?
- How often do you change language and literacy centers?
- How should you handle accountability and assessment of work at language and literacy centers?
- How are language and literacy centers implemented in the upper grades?
- How many language and literacy centers are needed?

Language and literacy centers are an essential element to the balanced literacy classroom. Diller (2003) defines literacy centers as small areas within the classroom where students work alone or in small groups to explore literacy activities while the teacher provides small-group and guided reading instruction. Centers or stations

A language and literacy center could easily be created on the book The Life and Times of a Drop of Water *by Angela Royston using CCSS in a variety of activities, such as finding facts and opinion, problem solving, and evidence-based writing and summarizing.*

can introduce a new skill, concept, or idea, or they can be used to reteach or reinforce a skill. Further, Falk-Ross (2011) describes the functions of centers as a place "for practicing with reading elements, experimenting with reading strategies, activating independent monitoring and problem solving, providing extended time for reading, initiating reader response through writing, and allowing time for peer conferencing." Peer conferences can be about books read and writing completed. Once center routines are established, students can work at their own pace. Clear and concise directions for each activity are important so students know exactly what they are to accomplish at each center. Having a well-managed and maintained system for center assessment helps the students learn management and organization within the community. Keep a checklist at the center so students are reminded of everything they need to complete before moving to the next center.

What makes the new language and literacy centers different is that there is a clear focus on children solving problems at the centers while working on teams. There is deliberate attention on students building arguments and finding evidence within the activity. Stout (2009) discusses centers as a way to create socially based learning, which could encourage the discourse and rich conversation. Informational and nonfiction books are featured at the centers.

Literacy Centers: Key Points

- Language and literacy centers are areas designed for a specific learning purposes (literacy needs of students).
- Literacy-appropriate materials enable learners to explore and work independently and in small groups.
- Language and literacy center activities should allow for open-ended inquiry.
- Language and literacy centers engage students in tasks as active learners.
- Language and literacy centers can provide students with choice in activities.
- Language and literacy centers are part of the daily ongoing classroom routines.

What's New? At-a-Glance: The New Language and Literacy Centers

- The language and literacy centers focus on students solving problems on their own and with others.

- Centers are used as a place for students to engage in 21st-century research and communication tools.
- Centers encourage students to raise important issues while doing their work.
- Students write research-based reports at centers.
- Centers take place in all the disciplines including art, music, and physical education.
- While working with others at centers, students generate rich discussion and conversation.
- Students learn to build arguments at centers.
- Students learn the skill of persuasion while working with others and in teams at centers.
- Language is in action at centers where social discourse permeates.

Teacher Tips for the New Language and Literacy Centers in All Grades

- Create centers that are attractive and inviting for conversations with a partner and with teams.
- Create objectives and student directions that are clear and easy to follow with a built-in management and assessment system.
- Create opportunities for students to think, work, and converse using higher-order thinking skills and/or academic vocabulary.
- Create centers offering opportunities, not only for conversations but rigorous discourse.
- Create assessments and/or means to document the conversations and work.
- Create extensions and modifications for enriching instructions as well as supporting students who struggle.

Teacher Tips for the New Language and Literacy Centers in Grades Five through Eight

- Create centers that support both reading and writing in all the content areas, including poetry.
- Create centers that have fiction, nonfiction, and challenging texts.
- Create centers that ask students to support their work with evidence and encourage students to work in teams or with a partner.
- Create centers that have students develop arguments and work in teams.
- Create centers that have students compare and contrast multiple texts.
- Create centers that are portable and function for both individual and team use.

The New Independent Reading and Writing

Guiding Questions:

- What is new about the independent reading and writing?
- How does independent reading and writing happen in all disciplines?

Independent reading that offers adult support, embedded instruction, and a student focus holds real potential for student reading growth (Sanden, 2012). The new emphasis on students reading more in disciplinary subjects and the new requirement that students explain their reasoning, particularly through writing in those same subjects, requires that teachers become familiar with reading and writing across the curriculum. This includes reading and writing in art, music, and science. Thus, managing both reading and writing independently will take on a new shape in classrooms.

Characteristics Of A good Parent

To be a good Parent is most important today. Parents must have certain characteristics to be a good Parent. I think the three most important are to be Patient, Domestic, and amusinG. the

When mY Parents are Patient, It means theY listen and give me more time. For example when I'am doing Something, like mY Homework, And wheh Iam talKing With mY friends, These are times when mY parents are are Patient with me.

When mY Parents can be amusinG to me I think it is A good thing. LiKe telling stories or funny joKes. MY Mom tells me a bedtime story every night Something when theY try to be funnY or amusinG, theY don't make me laugh. the times theY do, are just with MY friends. I reallY think theY can be funnY.

I Put Domestic down because mY Parents aren't home alot. they work alot. I wish theY alwaYs wouldn't have to work so much so I could be with them more. Somtimes, on school daYs, theY could both be home when I get home.

A student writing sample of building an argument for what makes a good parent

Reading and writing are firmly tied together, and writing instruction is explicit in the new Common Core (Gewertz, 2012). The expectation that students base more of their analysis on the text requires deeper investigation from them and a different set of strategies taught by teachers. Within CCSS is a call for all teachers, including those teaching science, social studies, history, and other subjects, to develop strategic instruction around literacy skills unique to their discipline. Students will be required to read and understand texts with greater degrees of complexity. The new independent reading and writing model is in perfect alignment with this expectation because the model promotes the use of authentic classic and contemporary literature (fiction, nonfiction, and poetry) to teach the standards. This selection of literature can be seen in the development of the CCSS exemplar texts. While the inclusion of more nonfiction to increase reading beyond traditional literature is a marked change for teachers, our balanced literacy model has always emphasized the reading of complex texts. The new model embraces fully these new standards in both reading and writing.

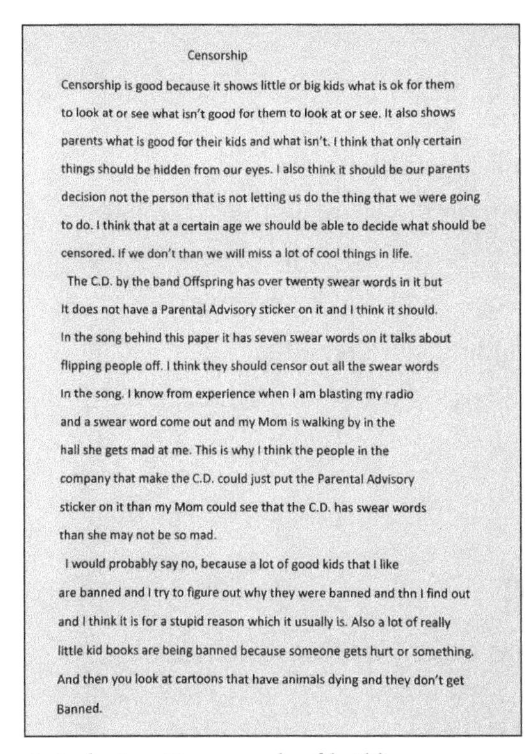

Censorship

Censorship is good because it shows little or big kids what is ok for them to look at or see what isn't good for them to look at or see. It also shows parents what is good for their kids and what isn't. I think that only certain things should be hidden from our eyes. I also think it should be our parents decision not the person that is not letting us do the thing that we were going to do. I think that at a certain age we should be able to decide what should be censored. If we don't than we will miss a lot of cool things in life.

The C.D. by the band Offspring has over twenty swear words in it but It does not have a Parental Advisory sticker on it and I think it should. In the song behind this paper it has seven swear words on it talks about flipping people off. I think they should censor out all the swear words in the song. I know from experience when I am blasting my radio and a swear word come out and my Mom is walking by in the hall she gets mad at me. This is why I think the people in the company that make the C.D. could just put the Parental Advisory sticker on it than my Mom could see that the C.D. has swear words than she may not be so mad.

I would probably say no, because a lot of good kids that I like are banned and I try to figure out why they were banned and thn I find out and I think it is for a stupid reason which it usually is. Also a lot of really little kid books are being banned because someone gets hurt or something. And then you look at cartoons that have animals dying and they don't get Banned.

A student writing sample of building an argument for censorship

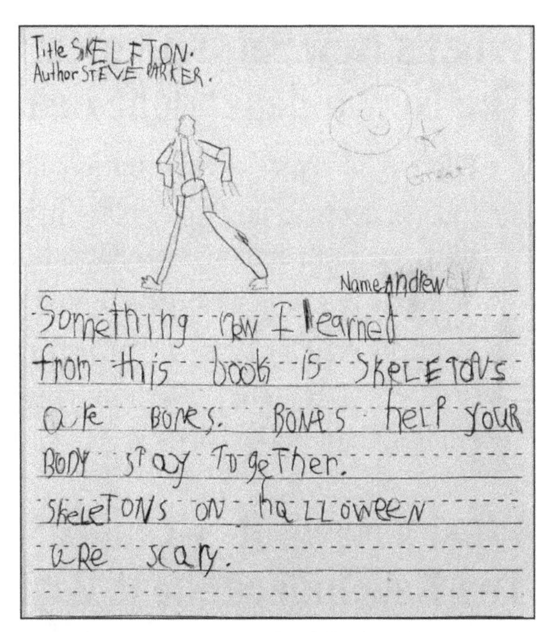

Title SKELETON.
Author STEVE PARKER.

Name Andrew

Something new I learned from this book is Skeletons are bones. Bones help your Body stay Together. Skeletons on halloween wre scary.

A student writing sample of finding facts from text

Don't Forget about the Narrative

Despite the push away from narrative in reading and writing to make room for informational and complex texts as well as persuasive and argument writing, there is still space for the narrative. Children's life stories need to be celebrated, appreciated, and most importantly, documented. Documentation comes in many forms: Diaries, journals, photos, and scrapbooks can all tell the stories of our lives. The life cycle of the memoir is represented below.

We can tell or dictate our stories, draw our stories, act out our stories, and write our stories through logs, journals, diaries, and memoirs. These precious documents show pieces of our lives and eventually the complete autobiography that develops over a lifetime of experiences. The personal narrative or memoir allows for the story of our life to unfold: self-examination of experiences in the highest form. Our narratives are always changing and evolving; they are a timeless search for meaning, recording our history. Indeed, all children and adults need to cultivate the skills to compose their own stories—especially the story of their own life. So while there is an ever-important push toward writing to show evidence from text and make arguments, there should certainly be room for the narrative in classrooms.

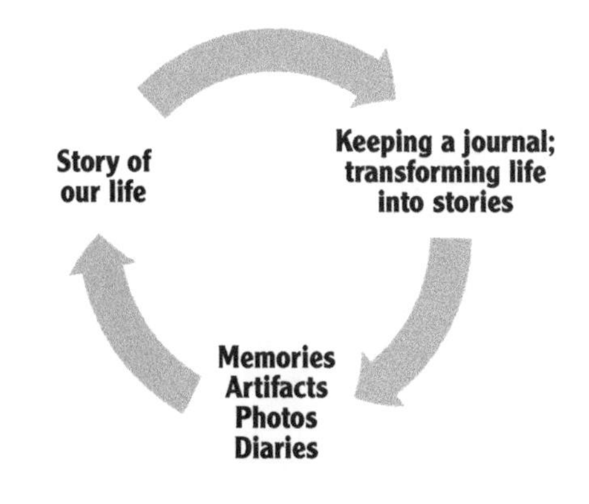

What's New? at-a-Glance: The New Independent Reading

- There is a balance of informational and disciplinary literacy texts.
- Independent reading takes place in all content areas, including art, music, science, math, and physical education.
- Students read complex texts to find evidence and build knowledge.
- Students read for different purposes, including close reading.
- Students read higher-level and more challenging texts during independent reading than in the past.

What's New? at-a-Glance: The New Independent Writing

- The time allotted for students during independent writing is increased.
- Independent writing should take place in all content areas, including art, music, math, science, and physical education.
- Independent writing should build students' knowledge of language and language conventions for writing.
- Independent writing time is used to develop opinion and persuasion in written work.
- Both informative and explanatory pieces along with narratives are focused on.
- Students participate in shared and peer research and writing.
- Students use text sources to find evidence to inform or make an argument.
- Students compare and contrast in their writing.
- Students use a variety of digital tools to produce and publish their writing during independent writing time.
- Students develop written responses from discourse.

The New Classroom Library

Guiding Questions:

- How do I create a classroom library that meets the new CCSS?
- How do I create a classroom library for the art, music, or physical education class?

Once again, access to books remains center stage in balanced literacy schools. Within the classroom, access is seen as a main factor that helps motivate students to read. Gambrell (2011) explains that when students have access to a wide variety and range of reading materials, they are more motivated to read. She further suggests that the range of materials should include an array of genres, text types, Internet resources, and real-life documents.

The bridge to the development and creation of a classroom library can be a daunting task for a classroom teacher with little or no experience. This section will guide new and veteran teachers and administrators into assisting all who begin to create classroom and other libraries within schools. Serafini (2011) discusses the idea of creating spaces in classrooms that emulate what the best bookstores have done by providing a relaxing setting, offering assistance, displaying books for easy access, promoting new selections, and making appropriate recommendations that are personalized for each reader. We also believe it is important to have students assist in the creation and management of the classroom library. Jones (2006) proposes having children involved in the process of setting up the library. She found that when students are involved and take ownership in the development of a classroom library, it increases the number of books they will eventually choose to read.

Throughout our years creating balanced literacy schools, it has been very rewarding to see a math, physical education, art, or music teacher get excited about balanced literacy. Some of the most interesting classroom libraries that have been developed come from these content areas. We saw a physical education teacher who had an amazing library on a cart in the gym. He began each class session with a read-aloud and actually gave kids a chance to read independently in class. What did his classroom library have? He had books about sports, wellness, health and fitness, and, of course, sports heroes. An art teacher had a collection of books about artists and the children read these books as part of independent reading time, which then evolved into doing research and reports on specific artists.

Diversity in the classroom library is an important factor to consider. Harris (2012) suggests a focus on books that reflect the ideas and experiences of African Americans, Asian-Pacific Americans, Latinos, and Native Americans. She also recommends books that include topics examining issues of disability, LGBTQ, class, gender, religion, and language. Further, these books should be exemplars of excellence.

If we want our students to be career ready, then we need to expose them to different cultures, so they will be able to communicate and interact with those outside their own culture. It is easier to interact with people that are different from you when you know something about their culture and their traditions. Exposure to different cultures through books is an easy initial means of introducing students to different societies and civilizations. By exposing children to diverse cultural literature, the implicit message is that the classroom is open to equal opportunity. Classroom libraries should reflect diversity. Children will feel welcomed by seeing their culture represented in these literary selections and will thus be more willing to discuss their culture with their peers and teacher. Parents who see their culture being valued by books in the school and classroom will feel more comfortable and willing to support the school. Displaying and reading literature that reflects students' membership in the classroom creates opportunities for discussions to compare and contrast different cultures. An example of how to accomplish this is through multicultural author studies. Here are some authors to consider:

- Alma Flor Ada
- Patricia Polacco
- Faith Ringgold
- Pam Muñoz Ryan

There are many other authors, and you can find writers that reflect the diversity of your room and that will expose students to different cultures.

Literature that focuses on a variety of social issues can also foster diversity while offering complex text choices:

- Social justice
- Anti-bullying
- Creating cultures
- Jealousy
- Puberty
- Religion
- Adolescence
- Racial tension

Literature that reflects important issues and is classic or award winning supports rigorous literacy conversations and inspires writing. This type of literature enables students to write arguments, collect evidence, and think deeply because the texts are usually well written and the student can see how other authors tackle issues or organize their thoughts. This rich literature serves as a model for many types of writing. The following sources for literature are good places to start:

- Appendix B in the Common Core State Standards
- Coretta Scott King Book Award winners
- Pura Belpré Award winners
- Caldecott Medal winners
- Newbery Medal winners
- Jane Addams Peace Association Children's Book Award winners
- Capstone Books

What's New? at-a-Glance: The New Classroom Library

- The new classroom library is organized so students can easily engage in independent reading and writing from a variety of texts.
- The new classroom library is seen in all content areas, including math, science, art, and music.
- The new classroom library offers books at demanding reading levels that will challenge students to read above their independent levels.
- 50 percent of the library collection in kindergarten through fifth grade should be informational and complex or challenging text.
- 70 percent of the library collection in grades six and up should be informational and complex or challenging texts.

Teacher Tips for Filling the New Classroom Library

- Garage and yard sales often include cheap books.
- Used book stores always have a treasure trove of finds.
- Dollar stores have a surprising selection of kids' books.
- Public libraries often have used kids' books on sale for as low as 10 cents.
- Charity and thrift shops are other places to find good used books.
- Always be on the lookout for bargain books at bookstores and online retailers.

A Teacher Resource for Social Justice Literature in the Classroom Library

According to the organization's website, the Jane Addams Peace Association Children's Book Awards have been given annually since 1953 to children's books published the previous year that "effectively promote the cause of peace, social justice, world community, and the equality of the sexes and all races as well as meeting conventional standards for excellence." Visit the website for fiction and nonfiction selections with a special emphasis.

What Does Summer Reading Look Like in a New Balanced Literacy School?

Guiding Questions:

- Why is reading during the summer important?
- How is reading supported during the summer for children?
- How do we provide access to books during the summer?

For 26 summers, we have had a reading clinic at Roosevelt University that provides the clinical practicum for our master's students. And for 26 summers, we have seen how important this clinic is for the children in the community. Many have come for their entire elementary careers, and parents have reflected that it made all the difference for students' success during the academic year. We have always known that summer reading is a crucial factor for overall academic success. It was our clinic work in the summer that helped inform our work in creating balanced literacy schools. This work resulted in adding the important aspect of access to books year-round to our balanced literacy school model. Typically, schools commit to offering a nine-month rather than year-round access period to books. Allington (2013) has written about the reading loss that can occur over summer when children are not enrolled in school. He further points out that summer reading loss is a compelling explanation for the widening gap between higher and lower socioeconomic status (SES) children in reading achievement. Our balanced literacy model begins with access to books for children year-round. Lindsay (2013) argues that access to books is especially important during the summer when children are unable to obtain books from their classroom. His meta-analysis indicates that children who have greater access to print material are more likely to have better attitudes towards reading, be more motivated to read, read more, have better language development, show stronger emergent literacy skills, demonstrate stronger reading and writing skills, and exhibit better overall academic achievement. These findings support year-round access to books for children. The need to strengthen the commitment to summer reading is critical.

When we first began summer reading initiatives, we encouraged all teachers to send books home for summer reading. Although ambitious, this was not as successful as we had hoped as there was no way to follow up or account for what happened after the books left the schools. More recently, we have assisted schools in developing a summer reading initiative (SRI)—a real plan for each school. What we now know is schools that develop an organized plan to carry out summer reading initiatives have success. We also know that when there is a designated time and place on a weekly basis for the children to come, they will come and check out books. The following list details some of the structures and ideas developed for the summer initiatives. (See Appendix C for more on summer reading initiatives.)

What's New? at-a-Glance: Summer Reading Initiatives

- A shift in thinking about summer reading accountability will need to happen in order to get schools and school leaders to take responsibility for providing access to books year-round.

Tips for Summer Reading Initiatives

- The literacy team and grade-level teams should discuss ideas for a summer reading initiative.
- Strong support is needed school-wide for the success of a SRI.
- Plan for a weekly visit to the school for book pickup by the children.
- Establish a central location and time for book checkout.
- Alternate morning and afternoon visits to accommodate student and parent schedules.
- The parent library, cafeteria, front entrance, outside school entrance, and playground all work well as accessible meeting spots.
- Have an incentive program in place for those that participate.
- Work with your public library on special arrangements like a weekly bookmobile visit to the school over the summer.

Chapter Three: Creating the Literate Environment

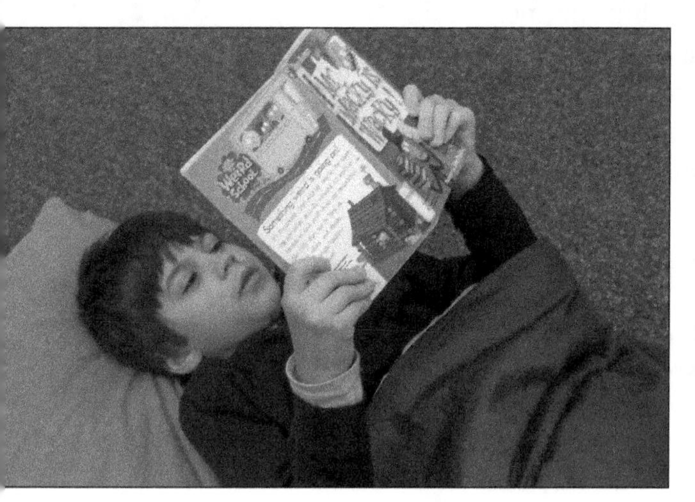

Creating a literate environment is essential to the success of school-wide literacy. Standard 5 of the International Reading Association's *Standards for Reading Professionals* (2010) describes the literate environment as a place where teachers foster reading and writing, including traditional print and digital and online reading and writing achievement by integrating foundational knowledge, instructional practices, approaches and methods, curriculum materials, and the appropriate use of assessments. This environment meets the needs of diverse learners while facilitating connections across all content areas as well as the world outside of school.

Guiding Questions:

- What does a safe, low-risk literate environment look like?
- What is the classroom routine like?

What Does a New Balanced Literacy Classroom Look Like?

The new balanced literacy classroom is designed uniquely to meet the instructional shifts and demands for a different kind of learning that is an outgrowth of the Common Core State Standards. The environment reflects the needs of the students to work in teams and collaborate on projects. Space that allows students to work independently and in groups should be considered along with places for read-alouds, shared reading, guided reading, and center work.

Designing the Physical and Social Environment

In the space below, design your classroom environment and include areas for the new read-alouds, new guided reading, word walls to language walls, language and literacy centers, independent reading and writing, and a new classroom library.

Space for read-alouds
Rocking chair and carpet
Space for classroom library
Space for guided reading and small-group reading lessons
Space for language and literacy centers
Quiet space for independent reading and writing
Social space for children to engage in conversation
Desks arranged for collaborative student work
Space for a listening center
Optional spaces for drama, art, and music
Space for 21st-century research/communication

What does a safe, low-risk environment mean?

Describe your social classroom environment, and include examples of the psychological, social, and emotional support given to learners as they expand their literacies. Include the "invisible" supports that you provide in your classroom literate environment.

What literacy learning takes place in your environment that extends beyond the classroom to explore literacy that affects the world?

What Does Classroom Instruction Look Like in the New Balanced Literacy Classroom?

Routines to Support Daily Reading and Writing Workshop

Routines are a critical component to a balanced literacy classroom. Having a daily routine allows for the children to anticipate and know what each day will be about. This organizational framework helps students have a natural flow that they can count on in the learning community and feel comfortable as they know what to expect during the day.

Sample Classroom Routines: What's Happening in Here Today?

The classroom routine is posted outside the classroom in the hallway for public and transparent viewing. The routine here is clearly stated and begins with a read-aloud and word wall and then moves into guided reading and literacy centers and stations. Times are posted so the routine is clear to the entire school community. Routine specifics can be erased and changed on a daily basis. In the new balanced literacy school, transparent practices are an important feature to capacity building and overall collaboration within the community. Posting the schedule in a public manner sends an important message about what is happening within the school. When children see a routine posted outside a classroom, they get a sense of what is happening inside. In one school, all the teachers have a template that is posted outside their classroom door that features the daily read-aloud, sending a strong message that this is an important part of the daily routine. As we strive for collective capacity building, teacher practices must become more public and transparent. Shared agreement about practices is essential.

A Template for 110 Minutes of Daily Balanced Literacy

The 110 Minutes of Daily Balanced Literacy routine evolved out of working with principals who, time after time, wanted a mechanism to know that the tenets of balanced literacy were happening in the classrooms. They wanted to be able to walk through the halls of their schools and know that read-alouds, guided reading, centers, and independent reading and writing were performed daily. As these conversations grew, it was clear that principals also wanted these routines to be shared and public. Thus, the 110 Minutes routine was created as a landscape-oriented sheet with two templates per sheet, where teachers could tear off one template (half a page), fill in the basics of each tenet, and post it outside their classroom. We are providing a similar template at right.

A sample journal reflects independent writing

This template serves as a guide for setting up a balanced literacy classroom routine. The schedule begins with 20 minutes of daily read-alouds and journal entries. The next 30 minutes are for whole-group instruction. This would be a time when a new skill or content is introduced to the entire class as a whole. After whole-group instruction, the teacher then works with three small groups of students for 20 minutes each. These groups rotate every 20 minutes so the teacher is able to differentiate instruction while working with a group of only five or six children at a time. The first group is the guided reading group. While the teacher meets with the guided reading group, the other two small groups work at literacy centers, independent reading or sustained silent reading (SSR), or research and writing. The non-guided reading groups are flexible and have choices within the learning environment. We want students to have independent time during the classroom routine for both reading and writing activities. Children need to count on sustained reading and writing time, during which they can read silently and do their daily writing, write in their journals, or continue ongoing research. This flexible time can also be for children to work together on projects. The management of the classroom routine takes time to develop and establish. In schools where routines are established in kindergarten, teachers and children develop habits more easily and look forward to and expect the established routines in each grade.

The week-at-a-glance format (shown after the template page) is especially helpful when planning a unit because it allows the teacher to see connections over a week and plan what books will be needed for read-alouds, what the journal entry will entail, what mini-lessons will be taught during whole-group instruction, how guided reading groups will work, how centers will rotate, and how to manage centers for each unit of study.

Date: ____________________

110 Minutes of Daily Balanced Literacy

Read-Aloud & Journal Entry – 20 min.

____
____
____
____

Whole-Group Lesson – 30 min.

____
____
____
____

Small Group: Guided Reading, Book Club – 20 min.*

____
____
____
____

Small Group: Language and Literacy Centers – 20 min.*

____
____
____
____

Small Group: Independent Reading and Writing – 20 min.*

____
____
____
____

*Small-group instruction rotates every 20 minutes.

Date: ____________________

110 Minutes of Daily Balanced Literacy

Read-Aloud & Journal Entry – 20 min.

____
____
____
____

Whole-Group Lesson – 30 min.

____
____
____
____

Small Group: Guided Reading, Book Club – 20 min.*

____
____
____
____

Small Group: Language and Literacy Centers – 20 min.*

____
____
____
____

Small Group: Independent Reading and Writing – 20 min.*

____
____
____
____

*Small-group instruction rotates every 20 minutes.

110 Minutes of Daily Balanced Literacy: Week at-a-Glance

	Monday	Tuesday	Wednesday	Thursday	Friday
Read-Aloud & Journal Entry – 20 min.					
Whole-Group Lesson – 30 min.					
Small Group: Guided Reading – 20 min.*					
Small Group: Literacy Centers – 20 min.					
Small Group: SSR and Writing – 20 min.					

*Small-group instruction rotates every 20 minutes.

What Does Assessment Look Like in a New Balanced Literacy Classroom?

Guiding Questions:

- What is ongoing and informal assessment?
- What is a running record?

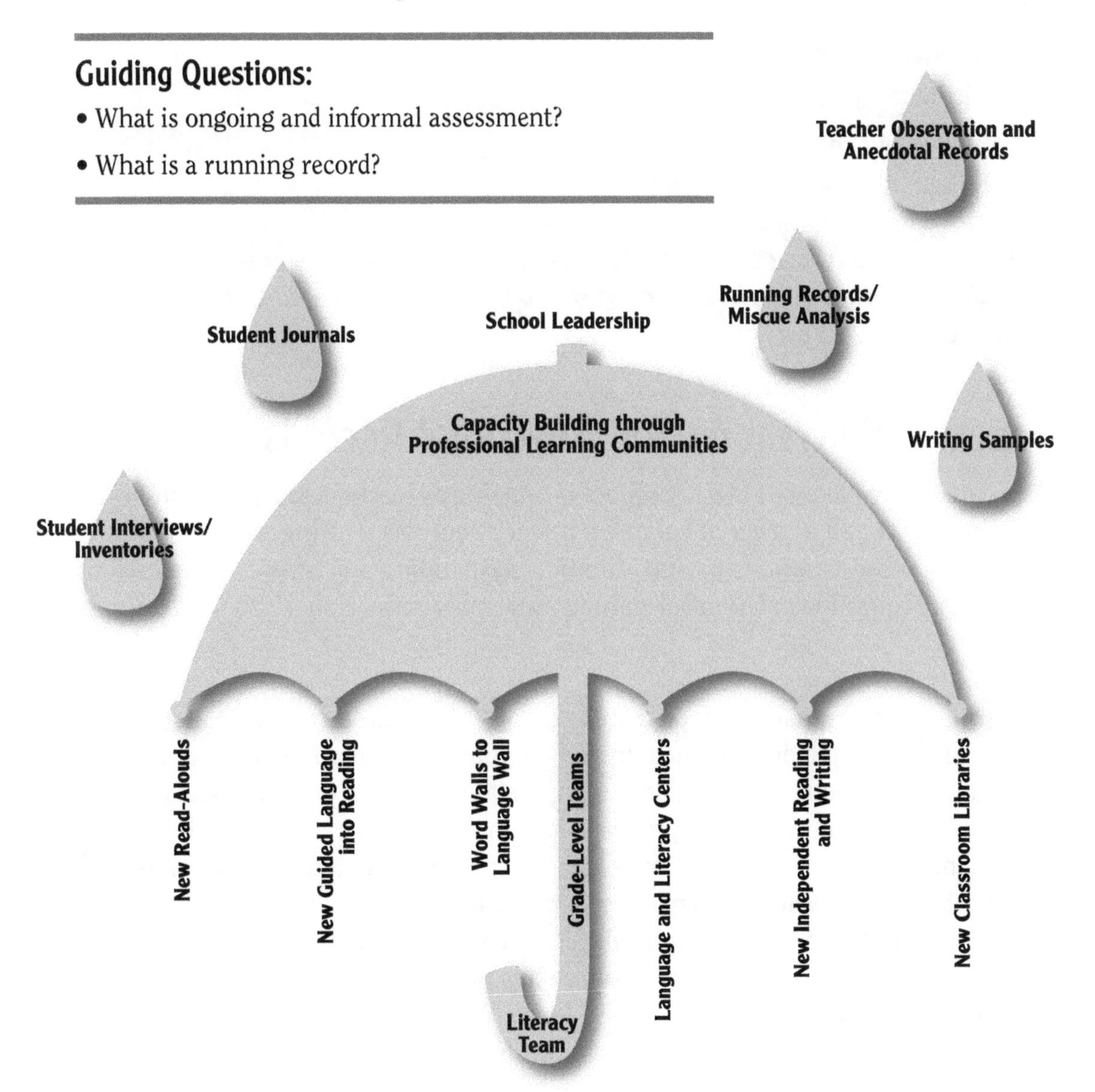

Our balanced literacy umbrella model uses raindrops to include all areas of assessment in a new balanced literacy classroom. Each raindrop represents a dimension of assessment. For example, the drops can include teacher observation and anecdotal notes, running records, etc. We think of assessment as an ongoing part of the daily routine. Further, assessment and instruction are seen as merging processes within classrooms. Assessment is a critical component of the decision-making process within balanced literacy. To support teachers in their decision-making process, data needs to be collected systematically. The goal of this data collection is to document change over time (Clay, 2001) as well as gather evidence of learning (Shea, Murray, and Harlin, 2005). In a balanced literacy school, informal assessments like those on the next page can provide objective data for instruction and be collected regularly.

- Teacher observation and anecdotal records
- Running records/miscue analysis
- Writing samples
- Student journals
- Student interviews/inventories

Make sure you have a clipboard with you at all times so you can document students' literacy behaviors. Putting sticky notes on the clipboard is another way to keep observations.

Teacher Observation and Anecdotal Records

Assessment in a balanced literacy school is ongoing as teachers are always observing students during all aspects of balanced literacy routines. During a read-aloud, the teacher can observe who is paying attention, responding and answering questions, and asking questions. Overall listening and comprehension skills can also be assessed.

During the new guiding language into reading, teachers can observe small groups and document just about any reading and language behavior. Moreover, documenting the conversations and discourse is important. Observation and assessment of children working at centers will provide a lens into how children work both independently and with peers on teams. Problem-solving, argument, and persuasion skills can be observed as well. Independent reading and writing provides the teacher with a special time to observe what habits children have gained and are developing. Taking observation notes and records on a daily basis offers planning tools and guidance for the next instruction needed for each child. We encourage teachers to use a clipboard for taking observational notes. Sticky notes with the student's name and date are one easy way to document observations on student progress with skills, interesting conversation and discussion points, questions or inquiry raised, and any behaviors that indicate the need for more guidance. These notes are then recorded as part of the anecdotal record, which contributes to students' overall formative assessments.

Running Records/Miscue Analysis

A running record is a written record of a child's oral reading that informs a teacher about that child's reading behavior (Fountas and Pinnell, 1996). Running records are used to record the reading behaviors on new text, familiar text, fiction, or nonfiction. The data gathered can inform as well as support decisions about grouping and instruction. In addition, a child's reading behaviors can be recorded across all texts used in a curriculum so that an overall picture of the child's ability to read and comprehend information can be gathered and used as evidence of learning across the disciplines. This type of informal assessment is suited for all genres and grade levels, so records can be assembled over a student's school career. But the unique and powerful value of running records is the immediacy of the assessment and the determination of a student's strengths and weaknesses through scoring and analysis.

Running records are sometimes used as only a one-time reporting mechanism for determining a child's level of reading. However, these records should instead be taken frequently, allowing teachers to learn about a child's different patterns of correct reading, errors, and metacognitive behaviors. This examination of the errors makes running records very similar to another informal assessment called miscue analysis (Goodman, 1969). With both types of informal assessments, the errors or miscues have a logic of their own that can convey insight into the child's thinking and reading process. The more samples a teacher takes, the more accurate the picture of a child's reading becomes. However, a teacher needs at least 20 experiences with taking, scoring, and analyzing running records or miscue analysis records to become comfortable and confident using these forms of informal assessments.

Writing Samples

These products from writing instruction can offer important data about students' writing competencies in such areas as idea generation, organization, style, and conventions. Like running records, writing samples go across all content areas and provide data that can be organized and used for instructional decisions. Teachers can analyze the work of individual students, small groups, and a whole class and use the data for differentiating instruction. We strongly suggest that either grade-level teams or a school literacy team construct writing rubrics for different genres and/or grade levels for assessing writing samples. Rubrics standardize this informal assessment as well as provide information about student learning that can be more specifically adapted to learning objectives and outcomes. Rubrics also help define lesson objectives and make reporting a student's strengths and weaknesses easier within a classroom and across grade levels.

Not only can content-area teachers use this informal assessment, but students can assess their own writing and set goals for themselves. Writing samples are a basis for modeling and become authentic material for writer's workshop for a whole class, small group, or individual students. Writing craft, or traits, from the writing samples are highlighted by teachers in their read-alouds, so that students can see how published authors use these elements of craft in their writing.

Teachers can receive positive and useful feedback about their students' writing and instruction when they present writing samples during grade-level meetings. This process usually begins by having the literacy or the grade-level team create a format or protocol for discussing the student work. Prior to bringing students' work to a grade-level meeting, teachers assess the writing samples and divide them into three groups of high, medium, and low scores. Typically, a few minutes are given for all teachers within the grade-level team to view and consider the students' writing and then take notes about individual samples to specifically address during discussion time. Concentrating mainly on lesson objectives keeps the process and discussion positive and focused. And finally, sharing student work fits in well with the school-wide goal of having collective, transparent practices.

Arguments, informative/explanatory pieces, narratives, and other written work across the curriculum are all good writing samples to use for assessment.

Student Journals

Student journals are used during the 110 Minutes but can also be a source of data for teachers to periodically collect and evaluate. Here are some ideas for journal writing that can be assessed.

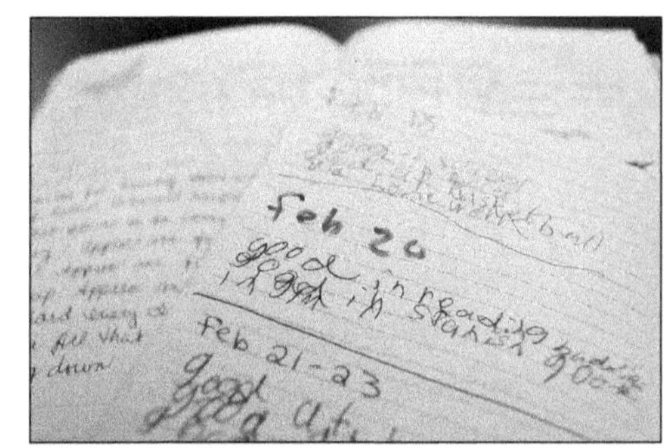

1. Reading logs: Allot several pages for students to add a list of books that have been read and books they want to read. The students write the title, author, and genre after they have read the book. Data from the logs provides information about the amount and genres read as well as student's favorite authors.
2. Response to reading: This includes students' responses to both fiction and nonfiction books. For more structured responses, the teacher or grade-level team can create a rubric. For example, this is a perfect time to have students include evidence to answer specific questions. The questions can become more complex, so the teacher can evaluate whether the child is capable of gathering evidence from texts independently.
3. Notes about books/reading strategies: This is also a good place for students to be reflective about what they are learning and/or their learning goals. Teachers can record the students' reflections and gain insight into their learning.
4. Vocabulary words: Students record interesting, important, and academic words found in their reading. Encourage students to use these words in future writing. Students write the word, an original definition, and the sentence from the text. Consider asking students to include a picture or diagram of the word. Later, teachers can review these words with all students. This personal and strategic dictionary is especially helpful for struggling readers and ELLs.

Student Interviews/Inventories

Interviewing students or administering reading/writing inventories can help teachers get to know their students better. There are many commercial models for interviews and inventories; however, teacher-created ones, in our opinion, are more effective because questions can be tailored to meet specific needs. Some basic questions that teachers usually ask students are:

- Do you like to read and/or write and why or why not?
- What is your favorite part of the day in school (besides lunch and recess)? Why?
- Do you read outside of school? If so, what types of books to you read?
- What is your favorite hobby?
- What books are you currently reading?
- What series or authors do you read or have you read?
- What type of writing do you like to do?
- What do you do when reading does not make sense or when you make an error/mistake in your reading/writing?
- Do you think reading is easy or hard? Why?
- Do you think writing is easy or hard? Why?

Emergent readers need additional assessments, which may cover these skills:

- Concepts about print
- Phonological awareness
- Phonics and word recognition
- Developmental spelling
- Fluency

Formal Assessment and CCSS

States will be moving away from a single formal assessment to several assessments for evaluating how students are performing with CCSS. To accomplish this task, states have grouped themselves into two consortiums: Partnership for Assessment of Readiness for College and Careers (PARCC) and Smarter Balanced (Achieve, 2012). A few states are in both consortiums. Both consortiums are devising and administrating formal standardized assessments that states will use in lieu of their state's formal assessment. Policy makers are hoping that the competition used with the two consortiums will support innovation; however, both consortiums are working with one another.

Both consortiums will use periodic assessments as part of their framework. PARCC's assessment framework will begin with a diagnostic test at the start of the year so that teachers will have an understanding of the strengths and weaknesses of their students. Then a mid-year assessment will be administered to check on student progress, and a final assessment at the end of the school year will be given. Smarter Balanced will also be offering optional interim tests at the beginning and mid-year point with a final assessment at the end of the year. PARCC requires testing in grades nine through 11, but Smarter Balanced makes this testing optional for those grades. After piloting the assessment, Smarter Balanced will determine its cutoff scores for passing or failing, but PARCC will set cut-off scores after the first year of implementation.

Both consortiums will be utilizing computer technology. According to its website, Smarter Balanced will have a computer adaptive testing (CAT) model, which has students taking assessments on computers that adjust the text difficulty and questioning during the assessment sessions. For example, if a student receives a correct answer or read a text correctly, then the student is later challenged with harder text and questions; however, if a child incorrectly answers the question or reads text incorrectly, then the child receives easier text and questions. The Smarter Balanced consortium believes that the assessment is tailored to the child so that it can evaluate which skills the child has mastered.

According to its website, PARCC's assessments are a fixed format for all students, so questions and text difficulty does not change during the session. The philosophy is that all students need to perform at grade level, so these assessments can give teachers and administrators a clearer picture of how a child is performing at that particular grade level.

PARCC Assessment (PARCC, 2012)

Each component will be computer-delivered and will use technology to incorporate innovations.

- Two summative, **required** assessment components designed to:
  - Make "college- and career-readiness" and "on-track" determinations,
  - Measure the full range of standards and full performance continuum, and
  - Provide data for accountability uses, including measures of growth.
- Two non-summative, **optional** assessment components designed to:
  - Generate timely information for informing instruction, interventions, and professional development during the school year.

- In English language arts/literacy, an additional non-summative component will assess students' speaking and listening skills. This component is required, but the score is not included in the summative score. This component will be locally scored.

The overall assessment system design will include a mix of constructed response items, performance-based tasks, and computer-enhanced, computer-scored items.

SMARTER Balanced (Smarter Balanced, 2013)

- **A summative assessment** is administered during the last 12 weeks of the school year. The summative assessment will consist of two parts: a computer adaptive test and performance tasks that will be taken on a computer, but will not be computer adaptive.
- **Optional interim assessments** are administered at locally determined intervals. These assessments will provide educators with actionable information about student progress throughout the year. Like the summative assessment, the interim assessments will be computer adaptive and includes performance tasks.

Both websites offer samples from their assessments.

What's New? at-a-Glance: Creating the New Literate Environment

- 110 minutes or more of literacy routines align with the new balanced literacy.
- Practices are public and shared both within and outside of the classroom to build capacity school wide.
- Assessment is ongoing now as teachers are observing the necessary shifts in learning for success in CCSS.

Teacher Tips for Creating the New Literate Environment

- Establish a routine like 110 Minutes of Daily Balanced Literacy (or more).
- Post this routine both inside and outside your classroom to make your practices transparent.

Chapter Four: Leadership and School-wide Literacy Initiatives

Guiding Questions:

- What does leadership look like in a new balanced literacy school?
- What is a school literacy team and how does it function?
- How do effective grade-level teams operate in a new balanced literacy school?

What Does Leadership Look Like in a New Balanced Literacy School?

Leadership to implement CCSS and all the known challenges that come with this task requires attention from the administration, which includes the principal, assistant principal, and other school leaders involved with literacy. This is a crucial time in education, as we don't have documentation from history for such grand and enormous reform. In order to carry out the important responsibilities in creating a new balanced literacy school, there are certain characteristics of quality leadership we have identified. When we first meet a principal, we are excited to begin a new partnership and relationship. Often, principals are not reading specialists, nor do they have the background and training in literacy. But these principals do make literacy a priority for their entire school in all grades and content areas. They are very welcoming and appreciate the support and assistance in literacy professional development.

Principals at new balanced literacy schools are strong decision makers, flexible in their thinking, and very interested in forming and shaping collaborative and cooperative structures within their schools. They know how to build and develop trust with all members of the school community, and they are kind and caring individuals who want the best instruction and learning taking place in their schools. They work hard and are tuned into their school. They know what is going on in each classroom. Mutual respect and shared decision making are authentic parts of the culture. Student learning is a top priority, and these principals care deeply about their teachers, devoting time and resources to their professional development.

These leaders take initiative to make the structural changes necessary for school-wide collaboration by developing both a literacy team and grade-level teams. Furthermore, they make it a priority to attend the meetings once the teams are established. Overall, we would identify these principals as strong leaders who are not afraid to take new risks, clear the playing field, and begin anew. In one school, the principal cleared out the teacher desks in each classroom and replaced them with guided reading tables. We thought this to be quite a bold move. The teachers actually appreciated it, and it gave them more space for the small-group instruction they were looking to do. Strong leaders make room for the new spaces needed to create new balanced literacy schools. They make spaces for the parent library and establish a room for the guided reading library, read-aloud library, and other libraries as well. They welcome the idea of hallbraries and embrace the transformation that takes place within the physical spaces of their building. Moreover, these leaders take ownership of the small and large endeavors and are proud of them. They assess and document the progress and celebrate the achievements with the learning community at large.

Excellent leadership in balanced literacy schools provides support for ongoing professional development for the teachers, investing in sending teachers to important conferences to increase their learning and stay up to date with all best practices. These principals find ways for teachers to have substitutes in order to attend a conference. Strong leaders support ongoing professional development through grade-level and literacy team meetings with rich conversations regarding best practices in literacy. With a focus on student learning and data during grade-level meetings, teachers are engaged in inquiry about student learning and often leave meetings gaining new understanding about their own pedagogy. Strong leaders also support peer observations, which result in teachers sharing practices and gaining new knowledge about pedagogy and implementation. Other support might include sharing an article or participating in a school-wide book club.

In one school, the principal developed a virtual professional learning community on a book about the Common Core State Standards where the teachers were able to respond to the text, post questions, and align what the book addressed to their own school and classrooms. The development of the virtual learning community grew out of the frustration of not finding enough time in the school day for this kind of discussion. This was welcomed by the teachers as they could respond at their own convenience.

We have also noticed that special leaders recognize professional development as career wide—there is no quick fix or magic bullet. Rather, they value and spend time outside of school for designated professional development, which includes evenings and weekends, and consider this time invested wisely.

Excellent leadership is not afraid of resistance to creating a new balanced literacy school, but rather, they welcome it and know how to work with it. They understand the challenges that major changes and transitions bring about in the culture of a school. Changing a school's culture takes time and investment, and these wise leaders are patient and diligent in their efforts. They understand there might be days when it feels as if they are going backward in their quest to make changes, knowing that this is normal for such a large-scale undertaking as creating a new balanced literacy school. These leaders know how to roll out new initiatives through school-wide collaboration and set clear priorities and deadlines for implementation. This is crucial for making and bringing about true school-wide change. The word "non-negotiable" is used in terms of what needs to get accomplished in the school and classrooms by a certain agreed-upon deadline. Finally, and most importantly, we observed that these leaders never seem to settle for mediocrity and are never satisfied with the status quo.

What Does Leadership Look Like in a New Balanced Literacy School?

- Leaders make literacy a school-wide priority in all classrooms and content areas.
- Leaders welcome support for professional development and value ongoing professional development for teachers.
- Leaders are strong decision makers, caring, trustworthy, and flexible in thinking.
- Leaders make physical and structural changes in the school necessary for balanced literacy.
- Leaders are not afraid to take risks and set priorities and deadlines for implementation of new initiatives.

The School-wide Literacy Team

Langer (2004) characterizes schools that are effective as welcoming, competent, collaborative, and professionally involved. In effective schools, students are mentally engaged in school content and see school as a place to learn and actively participate. Excellent schools don't just happen; rather, they require an enormous amount of professional development that is woven into the learning community and is seen as an ongoing cycle of learning and change for teachers, administrators and, of course, students. The school-wide literacy team and grade-level teams provide the perfect forum for ongoing professional development. This collaborative team model addresses the needs specific to their roles and responsibilities, working off the premise that all team members contribute to the overall literacy success of the school. Team development plays a critical role in capacity building at the school level as the training of team members in building collaboration is a key factor in determining the success of such a model to bring forth change (Booth and Rowsell, 2007).

The formation of a school-wide literacy team should be a priority for balanced literacy implementation and success. Literacy teams are important because they provide a channel for faculty to communicate openly and effectively and then report back to grade-level peers. An important aspect of a literacy team is developing an infrastructure through shared decision making, which can support meaningful and lasting change (Blachowicz et al, 2010). Literacy teams develop shared leadership, staff trust, and a feeling of personal responsibility (Lieberman, 2000). They also build the democratic structures needed to sustain successful change (Booth and Rowsell, 2007; Fullan, 2007).

Creating this team should involve input from the principal and the school reading specialist/coach. The literacy team should have a teacher representative from each grade level to allow for communication back and forth to the grade-level teams. Cobb (2005) explains that there is no one model for the formation of a literacy leadership team. She suggests that members include the principal, the reading specialist or literacy coach, a primary teacher, an intermediate-level teacher, and any resource teachers (bilingual or special education) who work with students across grade levels. If there is a school librarian, we recommend that he or she be on a literacy team.

The literacy team includes teachers from all disciplines. This is instrumental in making every teacher a teacher of literacy. By including everyone and not excluding anyone, the staff can become more focused and cohesive around a common vision of literacy. A literacy team cannot simply be announced and implemented but must proceed through consensus. Teachers must get experience in collaborating and developing trust. For this reason, literacy teams and grade-level teams need to implement in tandem so that these first steps in faculty governance occur simultaneously.

There are important practical considerations to establishing successful literacy teams:

- The time and place of the meetings need to be established with regularity.
- Teams need to meet either before or after school.
- Meetings should not exceed an hour.
- Teams should have a wide representation, both in terms of grade levels and types of teachers.

Team members may also need help in fostering communication skills. Creating a literacy vision for the school is a great first task. Strategies that are sometimes used in the classroom, such as Think-Pair-Share (Lyman, 1981), are helpful in getting team members to participate more and discover surprising strengths in their colleagues. A successful literacy team must be grounded in a healthy respect for a diversity of opinions. Team members need to feel comfortable contributing ideas without fearing criticism. As a literacy team matures, it develops a common language and shared understandings.

Below is a sample template for a literacy team meeting. A blank template appears on the next page.

Literacy Team Minutes

Date/Time: November 13, 2013; 3:00–4:00 p.m.

Mission/Purpose
The Dore Literacy Team will advocate and establish data-driven decisions to enhance student achievement. An emphasis on curricular planning, performance assessments, and student work will guide conversations and elicit high-quality instructional practices and tasks that will be disseminated through the grade-level teams. Highlighting purposeful and intentional best practices and student outcomes will determine future professional development, empowering the entire school community.

Today's Outcomes

Time	Topic
3:00–3:10	Read through teacher responses from November 1st PD 1. Why is purposing effective for students? 2. How are we going to measure that purposing the lesson is effective for our students?
3:10–3:40	Discuss ways in which we will measure student effectiveness in the classroom.
3:40–3:55	Come to final decision and write down specific goals, suggestions, and/or implementations.
3:55–4:00	Next week's agenda

Action Item	Owner	Due Date
Bring samples of purposing lessons to next meeting	All teachers	11/20

Roles for next meeting

Note Taker	Time Keeper	Facilitator		

Literacy Team Minutes

Date/Time:

Mission/Purpose

Today's Outcomes

Time	Topic

Action Item	Owner	Due Date

Roles for next meeting

Note Taker	Time Keeper	Facilitator		

What is a school literacy team?

Who is on a school literacy team?

What are the roles and responsibilities of the literacy team leader and members of literacy team?

What's New? at-a-Glance: The New Literacy Team

- The new literacy team develops professional learning communities to build capacity.
- The new literacy team sets forth a school mission that promotes the instructional shifts necessary for success in CCSS.
- The new literacy team focuses on student learning through collaboration and shared agreement among teachers.

Tips for Implementing the New Literacy Team

- Stay current with all new information regarding pedagogy and instructional shifts.
- Foster a culture of professional development that is ongoing.

Grade-Level Teams

High-functioning grade-level teams are essential to the success of a new balanced literacy school. Typically, grade-level teams have members from each grade represented. This model encourages all members from each grade to meet as a team. In schools where there are fewer classes in each grade level, the grade-level teams can be combined in order to meet more effectively.

Over the years, we have attended many grade-level meetings and seen that the function of grade levels varies greatly by school and district. For example, we often learn that grade-level teams conduct school business that should not be a part of grade-level planning time.

A Grade-Level Team Meeting Is Not for:

- Planning field trips, holiday celebrations, or class parties
- Dealing with student discipline issues and problems
- Socializing with peers
- Taking care of school business

A list of grade-level meeting norms and a template for taking notes at the grade-level team meetings are provided on the following pages.

Grade-Level Meeting Norms

(Adapted from Our Lady of the Wayside School)

Kindergarten

- Meet one day a week at lunch.
- Address academics first and end the meeting with housekeeping items.
- Agree to have a team leader to answer questions that arise.
- Focus on having a positive approach and share ideas and curricular activities.
- Meet twice a week once each month.

First and Second Grade

- Come prepared with agenda and specifics (student data and topics).
- Agree upon time to discuss each student brought to the meeting (use a timer).
- Stay on track, no sidebars.
- Remember to include some positives.

Third Grade through Fifth Grade

- Come prepared with an agenda and materials as needed (student data and topics).
- Agree upon time to discuss each student.
- Stay on track and follow agenda.
- Plan ahead and be prepared.
- Be open to suggestions, and be flexible.
- Share meeting responsibilities.

Middle School

- Come prepared with an agenda and student data.
- Show respect (of one another, no side conversations, be open minded).
- Have professionalism (i.e., be on time, on task, positive; show ownership; have all participate).
- Show fairness (i.e., all participate and contribute).
- Commit to implementation and follow through.

What would a schedule look like for grade-level teams to meet on a weekly basis?

What kinds of student data could be included at each grade-level meeting?

What roles and responsibilities would grade-level team members have?

Grade-Level Notes

Grade-Level Band	
Date/Time	
Location	
Attendees Present	
Grade-Level Manager	
Please Read/Bring	
Student Work Viewed	

Topic	Actions
Literacy Team	
Guided Instruction	
Assessment: Student Work/Data	
Learning Behavior Items	
Other/Next Week's Items	

What's New? at-a-Glance: The New Grade-Level Team

- Teams meet weekly and have a protocol that includes a central focus on student learning.
- Shared ideas about instructional shifts necessary for success in CCSS are discussed and agreed upon.
- The focus is on student learning and progress at all times.
- Professional development is built into the meetings; teachers share and collaborate on topics and read timely articles of interest.

Ongoing and Systematic Professional Development

Guiding Questions:

- How can professional development be built in to a school day?
- What is ongoing professional development?

Now, more than ever, an effort must be made to provide ongoing professional development for teachers. Gone are the days of one-day professional development for the year. School leaders must provide the opportunity for teachers to be in professional learning communities where new information and pedagogy is ongoing. Our goal is to have teachers learn about their craft throughout the school day.

We believe that capacity building can happen over time, and we have witnessed the transformation of schools—but only through ongoing professional development. To build capacity and keep up the momentum for school growth, professional development needs to be ongoing throughout the years (Fullan, 2007). Constant professional development enables teachers to work together toward a common goal over time. Teachers and administrators need time and opportunities to create a shared vision about their school's literacy instruction and student outcomes. To accomplish this, teachers and administrations need sustained time to learn how to work together, build trust, and problem solve. Through structured, ongoing professional development, we have seen administrators and teachers create professional learning communities (Eaker, DuFour & DuFour, 2002) and build capacity.

Carefully planned, continuous professional development needs to provide opportunities for discussion, but it also needs to be differentiated so that every staff member gets a chance to grow. A plan for incorporating new members or new teachers into the staff should also be developed. One part of our grant work is this new teacher induction. We believe it is important to include new teachers, incorporate them into the community of learners, and not have them feel isolated. Linda Darling-Hammond

(2010) explains that isolation is one of the main reasons teachers leave the profession. We have the literacy coach (Bean, 2009) bring the teachers together and educate the new ones about balanced literacy or help implement the model. New teachers need modeling, reassurance, information, and someone to listen to them. The literacy coach is a good person to do this because he or she is not an evaluator but has expert knowledge. The teacher is usually extremely appreciative and excited to have the support.

Many people say that this time and effort is unnecessary and not cost efficient, but neither is hiring new teachers year after year. The true payoff is that students get teachers who are continually improving and rethinking their instruction. In fact, some of the best, ongoing, all-staff professional development has occurred when we studied elements of balanced literacy and especially new balanced literacy over time. In addition, we include children's literature or professional books in almost every facet of our ongoing professional development. Teachers want professional development to have a purpose and to be useful. When someone places a children's book in a teacher's hands and shows her how to use that book, she tends to go back to the classroom and use the information immediately. Another outcome of using children's books or professional books is that it makes instructional practices more transparent.

The embedded, ongoing professional development in grade-level meetings is just one more approach that connects practice to action, and it helps teachers share their professional goals and growth in a more personal and intimate setting.

Chapter Five: Collaboration and Student Learning

Guiding Questions:

- What is school-wide collaboration?
- What is capacity building and what are its domains?
- What is a professional learning community (PLC)?

What Does Capacity Building Look Like in a New Balanced Literacy School?

In her article, "Leadership Roles in Implementing the Common Core State Standards," Massey (2013) states that the primary need for school leaders is to strategically plan the implementation of the CCSS for their schools. The task at hand is seen as understanding the standards and translating them into effective classroom practice while avoiding frustration and failure among teachers and students (Eilers and D'Amico, 2012). Capacity building, a rather new term for schools, includes the conditions and practices that support effective collaboration and impact student learning. Hargraves and Fullan (2012) discuss professional capital in much the same manner as the focus is on teachers collaborating on teams and realizing that the group is far more powerful than the individual. Implied in this quest to build capacity within schools is the notion that the teacher becomes a learner as well. This puts learning at the heart of all reform efforts and goes beyond students to include the system as a whole and those who work within it (O'Day, J., Goertz, M.E., and Floden, R.E., 1995).

Since there is not the reiteration of topics each year with the new standards, it is important that teachers across grades, and within grades, collaborate more effectively to ensure students are prepared each year for the next grade. This is especially necessary in the initial years of CCSS implementation. The school-wide teams (the literacy team and grade-level teams) created need administrative support to work in a collaborative manner. We propose that schools engage in capacity building through professional learning communities to meet these goals. Nace (2013) explains that the best investment leaders can make is to build capacity among staff members through the development of professional learning communities.

What Are the Domains to Implement Capacity Building?

A framework of six domains that support effective collaboration and impact student learning were developed (Nelson, Hill, Palmisano, Hebert and Roth, 2012). These domains provide research-based guidance for setting goals to improve professional collaboration and learning. We have added elements to the domains that support the development of balanced literacy. The six domains are as follows:

1. **Deprivatizing practice** includes both formal and informal peer observation on a regular basis; school-wide sharing for the accountability of student learning along with adult learning as a shared responsibility. Evidence is collected and comfortably discussed with others. Learning that occurs through collaboration is captured and shared with others. The 110 Minutes of Daily Balanced Literacy posted outside classrooms is one way to deprivatize practices.
2. **Enacting shared agreements** involves decision making and actions that focus on improving student learning in all content areas. All hold agreements about quality literacy instruction and how to effectively assess outcomes. Daily work and decision making are driven by these agreements. These shared agreements take place during grade-level meetings, where student learning is discussed and individual progress shared. Teachers engage in important conversations about pedagogy and best practice strategies in literacy.
3. **Creating collaborative culture** is done by having hard conversations that share both successes and failures safely and without judgment. Time for collaboration is used productively while sharing leadership and owning the process. Teamwork allows for a safe environment where teachers can talk about what has and hasn't worked in their classrooms. Teachers learn from each other when there is a collaborative culture.
4. **Maintaining an inquiry stance** means doing collaborative work that has clear goals and focuses on the core issues of student learning. Progress is closely monitored, commitments are made to act and report back to the group, and expertise is sought when needed.
5. **Using evidence effectively** centers on collaboration being grounded in evidence of student learning. Participants know how to use multiple sources of data, student work is examined regularly through grade-level team meetings, and actions are assessed in terms of impact on student learning.
6. **Supporting collaboration systemically** means dedicating time for professional collaboration. Work is supported by leadership, leaders provide data in a timely manner, and trying new ideas is encouraged. The concept of ongoing and systematic professional development permeates the culture of a professional learning community that is capacity building.

What Is a Professional Learning Community (PLC)?

One way to develop capacity building among teams is through the use of a professional learning community. Huffman and Hipp (2003) assert that a professional learning community (PLC) is "the most powerful professional development and change strategy available." Professional learning that increases educator effectiveness and results for all students occurs within learning communities committed to continuous improvement, collective responsibility, and goal alignment. Within professional learning communities, the team is the anchor or foundation for the collaborative work. Eaker and DuFour (2002) believe that the best hope for reculturing schools is the development of professional learning communities. This cultural shift begins with collaboration that moves a school from teacher isolation to collaborative teams. Eaker and DuFour state that there are four main priorities in a professional learning community:

1. Focus on student learning.
2. Focus on collaborative culture.
3. Focus on results.
4. Provide timely, relevant information.

We believe that these priorities are necessary to collaboration and capacity building. The focus begins with an eye on student learning, and this continues to take center stage in all facets of a balanced literacy school. Student learning inherently incorporates literacy learning and all the content areas. In professional learning communities, capacity is built through collaborative efforts that center on student learning. Once again, these collaborative efforts are built on teams, and the teamwork focuses on the results of student learning and progress. In professional learning communities, all data and information is reported so teachers and administrators can make decisions best suited for students and their progress.

On the following page, you will find a meeting log for a professional learning community grade-level meeting to assist you in your planning.

Professional Learning Community Grade-Level Team Meeting Log

Team: ______________________________ **Date:** ______________

Faculty/Staff Members Present

Team Meeting Guidelines Reviewed: Yes_____ No _____

Instructional Overview

1. Where are we in reading?
2. Where are we in writing?
3. Where are we in math?
4. Where are we in social studies?

Content-Area Focus: ______________________________

What do we want students to learn? (Look at instructional methods/strategies/best practices for upcoming topics and units.)

How will we know if they have learned it?

What types of assessments are being used to measure student learning and progress?

What types of assessments were discussed?

Are these common assessments? Yes No

Notes:

What will we do if the student did not meet the learning goal listed?

What interventions or strategies have you tried or will you try?

What will we do if students already met the learning goal listed?

What types of extensions and opportunities for change are in place?

What will we do to continue our learning?

Questions/concerns/professional development/support:

Chapter Six: Putting It All Together

Guiding Questions:

- Where does a school begin the process for developing capacity building?
- How does a school implement the framework that incorporates the new balanced literacy with Common Core?
- What role and responsibilities does a literacy coach have?

At a recent event sponsored by the Institute of Politics at the University of Chicago, U.S. Secretary of Education Arne Duncan said implementing the CCSS is "the most ambitious educational undertaking ever and will take four to five to 10 years to implement," (University of Chicago; October 24, 2013). In this final chapter, we hope to help you see how this ambitious task can indeed be implemented. In Chapter One, we discussed the need for the new balanced literacy model along with the new focus on language. Chapters Two and Three laid out all the characteristics and tenets of new balanced literacy as influenced by the necessary instructional shifts and how to set up learning environments and routines to support this instruction. Chapter Four detailed the necessary leadership and organizational structures, such as grade-level and literacy teams, that must be in place for a school-wide endeavor. Chapter Five made the case for school-wide collaboration through capacity building and the development of professional learning communities.

We now present a framework to assist schools—no matter where they might be in the process of implementing CCSS—with becoming new balanced literacy schools. We once again return to the balanced literacy model of an umbrella.

A Framework for Implementation of a New Balanced Literacy School

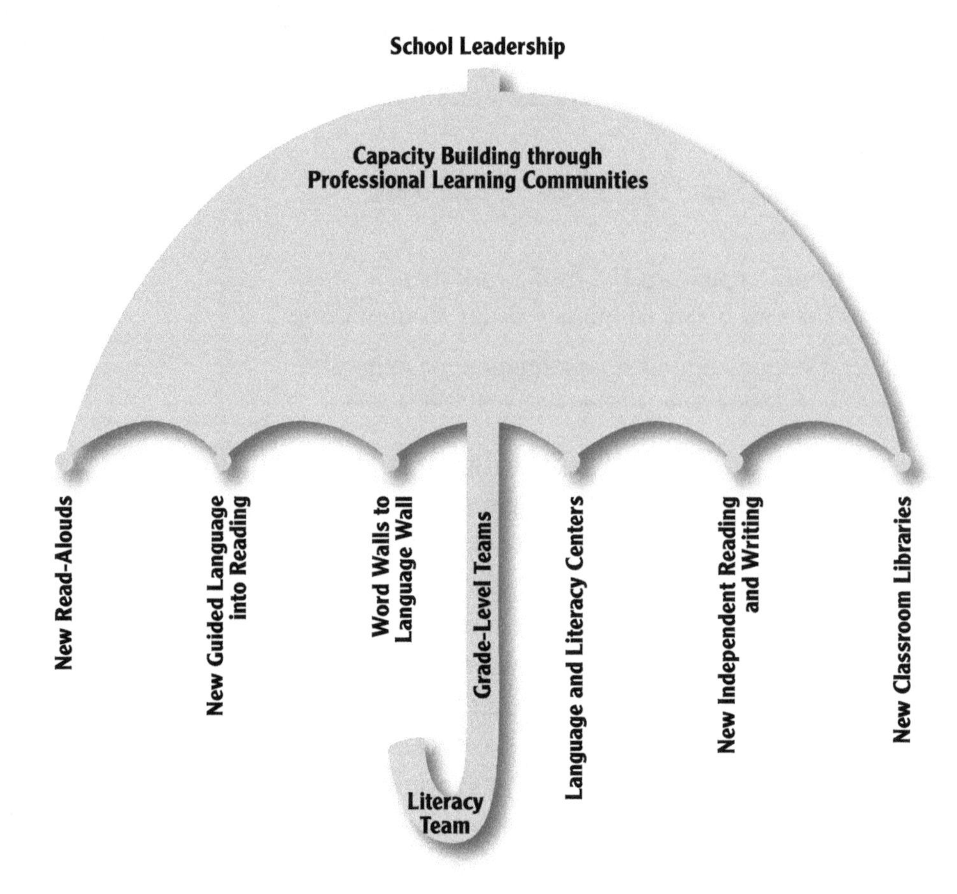

- The top (ferrule) of the umbrella represents the school leadership (principal, assistant principal).
- The hood of the umbrella represents the **capacity building through professional learning communities (PLCs)**.
- The six spokes of the umbrella represent the **six domains of capacity building.**
- Tips of the umbrella include (from left to right):
  1. Daily new read-alouds
  2. The new guiding language into reading
  3. Word walls to language wall
  4. Language and literacy centers
  5. New independent reading and writing
  6. Multiple in-school libraries, including classroom libraries
- The pole of the umbrella represents the grade-level teams.
- The handle of the umbrella represents the literacy team.

Where to Begin

Creating a new balanced literacy school begins at a school-wide level and moves to the team level, all along supporting teachers at the individual classroom level. This process can take many years to complete. We don't actually believe that the process is ever over as the professional development needs are continuous and ever changing. At the start, this can seem like an overwhelming and daunting task, both for administrators and teachers. Over and over again, we have seen schools regress after initial efforts were put forth. Often principals and literacy teams don't account for the time these kinds of major changes will take and set expectations too high. When change doesn't happen fast enough, it is not necessarily that things aren't working but rather that teachers need more time to assimilate and reflect on the shifts. These types of changes in school culture and practice take months and even years to happen. Our recommendation is that you start out by understanding that there will probably be some resistance. But persistence must win out in this journey! We suggest that you begin by developing a formal professional learning community (PLC) with a school-wide book club.

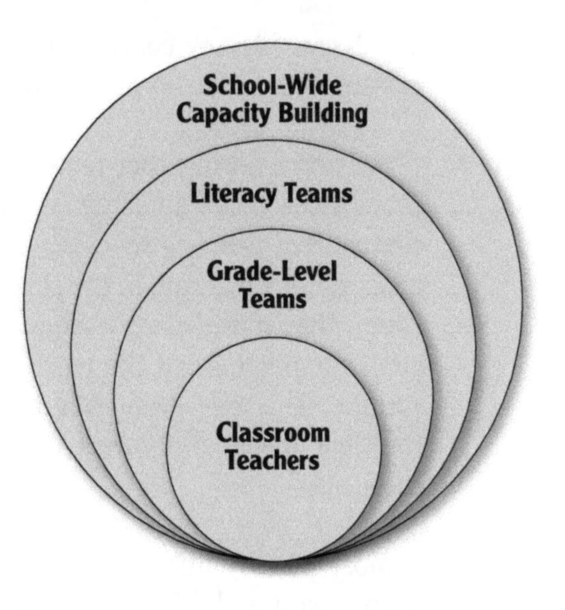

The cost associated with creating a balanced literacy school is always one of the first issues that needs to be addressed. We suggest that the literacy team first consider the books needed for multiple in-school libraries, which will cost very little in terms of actual dollars. If you do not have a literacy team, we suggest you establish one to begin the collaborative process and shared decision making that needs to be done. Here are some ways to initiate the process.

- Establish a school-wide literacy team to begin the process. Make sure you have the membership that will support all efforts.
- Take a school-wide inventory of all the books that belong to the school. This will give an accounting of what book resources already exist. Typically, schools have a strong collection of books; however, they need to be reorganized to give easy access to children, teachers, parents, and administrators.
- Centralize the guided reading and/or leveled books in a book room or balanced literacy room.
- Pull books from the school library (or make a space in the library) for the new read-aloud library.
- Take an inventory of all physical spaces in the school, and begin to think about where a parent library, read-aloud library, guided reading library, and novel sets library would serve the community best.

- Study the school entryway and determine the best location for the parent library.
- See Appendix B for more information on setting up a new balanced literacy school.

Literacy Coaching in the New Balanced Literacy School

The term "literacy coach" refers to a professional educator who collaborates with classroom teachers to provide individualized staff development (Cassidy et al, 2009).

Putting it all together requires many steps along the way. A reading specialist or literacy coach in your school is a nice asset to move the community along. When we first started working with schools to become balanced literacy driven, the literacy coaches were working in the classrooms to assist the classroom teacher. In the classroom, they modeled read-alouds and guided reading, helped in setting up literacy centers, and coached the teacher with the 110 Minutes of Daily Balanced Literacy routine. This role eventually expanded to other roles, which included developing multiple in-school libraries and facilitating the literacy team and grade-level team meetings.

Most recently, our emphasis has turned to capacity building school-wide. This has been a hard and difficult transition for teachers, coaches, and administrators. The unit of coaching is now focused school-wide on teams and capacity building. Literacy coaches must now reframe their thinking about how to still support classroom teachers while building capacity school-wide in literacy. This is no easy challenge; in fact, there has been resistance to this model. However, the school-wide focus remains and requires whole-school participation.

One way to think about moving from classroom to school-wide coaching is to think about how a sports coach operates. A sports coach works with the team as a whole and does not work in isolation with individual players. For example, imagine if a basketball coach worked in a separate gym with each player, assisting, modeling, scaffolding, etc. The player might improve skills, but the team as a whole would suffer terrible consequences on game day because the coach did not focus efforts on how the players could work together as a team. In schools, every day is like a game day where players must work in harmony and collaboration for the good of the students. Does this mean that the literacy coach or reading specialist is never in the classroom with the teacher? No. The coach still finds time to assist and work in the classroom, but it is in response to the literacy and grade-level team meetings and conversations. In this model, teachers are frequently visiting and observing each other's classroom so practices are shared, open, and public.

What's New? at-a-Glance: Coaching in a New Balanced Literacy School

- The focus of coaching is now school-wide to build capacity.
- Coaches work with grade-level and literacy teams to support the literacy mission of the school.
- Classroom teachers observe each other frequently and share their practices.

Introducing Parents and the Community to New Balanced Literacy

In new balanced literacy schools, parents are a critical and essential component. Literacy is a year-round endeavor in and out of the school, so parents need to be valued and play a role. Parent libraries, bedtime story routines, family literacy nights, workshops for parents, summer reading initiatives, and parent volunteer opportunities are some of the way parents can be engaged within a school.

Working with parents as partners is an important aspect of new balanced literacy schools. Often parents are not familiar with concepts and ideas of balanced literacy, so it is essential to provide the needed information for their understanding. Parents who do not know about balanced literacy and who might have had different educational experiences need to be assured that this is a best practice. Communicating information regarding the new balanced literacy model, along with the Common Core, is an important step in becoming a balanced literacy school. Schools will want parents informed about all the steps in the development and stages of the process. This will mean having several information events during the course of the year. Parent-teacher conferences are a good way for teachers to discuss the program with parents and also give tours of their classroom spaces. There are many other ways to communicate this process to parents. Some schools have used the following as an effective means to roll out their new balanced literacy model:

- A special back-to-school night
- Letters to parents
- Website information and updates
- A special meeting to introduce and discuss balanced literacy
- The launch of the parent library
- A special family literacy night where the parent library is introduced and an information session on balanced literacy is held

Depending on when and where you have your information session for parents, we encourage you to have the newly identified spaces clearly marked and labeled to show the work and progress you have made, making the practices both public and transparent.

For many years, we have sponsored parent workshop in our summer reading clinic. Initially, we were quite surprised at the large number of parents who attended. We then realized they valued getting some information, tips, and strategies to help their children with literacy. Our workshops have been successful and have gradually evolved over the years. When we first started the idea, we would invite only the parents (somehow we didn't figure in the children at that time). Now we invite the parents to bring their children and we make the workshop interactive with the children involved. For example, at a recent workshop about creating home libraries, the children helped design the spaces where they might create a library at home. The children in our workshops participate with parents and actually get a chance to try out what is being presented.

Tips for Running Parent Workshops

- If possible, offer them before school.
- Have them be no more than 30 minutes.
- Make them interactive in nature.

Ideas for Parent Workshops

- How to read aloud to your child each night and set up a bedtime story routine
- How to select just the right challenging book for your child for reading aloud at home
- Selecting informational and complex texts for your child
- Understanding Common Core State Standards and how parents can work with their children at home
- How to set up homework spaces and routines at home
- How to create a home library for family literacy
- How to use journals and diaries daily at home with your child
- How to make reading games at home with your child
- How to set up a word wall to language wall at home for your child
- The importance of summer reading at home with your child

Parents often are happy and eager to volunteer in their child's school. Setting up a new balanced literacy school requires enormous effort. We have had many of the parents in the schools we work volunteer precious hours toward the goal. They have assisted in setting up and managing the parent library, moving books and other materials out of rooms to make spaces for other new libraries, getting guided reading libraries set up by labeling bins, etc.

Jobs for Parent Volunteers

- Assist in the management of the parent library and other libraries.
- Clear out spaces to make room for the libraries.
- Read aloud to children near the hallbraries.
- Label bins for the guided reading library.
- Support summer reading initiatives (SRI).

Family literacy nights are another good way to keep families informed about the balanced literacy curriculum and also engage them in activities. This type of event can support and strengthen family literacy by offering opportunities for families to learn about reading aloud and other literacy strategies and activities. Reading activities at home help all family members—from grandparents to young toddlers—participate in literacy. Additionally, family literacy nights can celebrate activities, such as the bedtime reading so that parents and students will continue to have these informal yet powerful interactions at home.

How to Put a Family Reading Night Together

Usually the literacy team plans and organizes, with school-wide participation, the family literacy night. Involving more people in the planning will encourage collaboration. Many schools pick a theme for the family reading night, dress up as book characters, and even bring in storytellers. After the theme is chosen, a format is determined. One format that has been very successful is first having parents and students attend different breakout sessions in different classrooms or different parts of the gym. Then everyone gathers in the common space for a culminating activity like storytelling or a special talk about literacy. This format can also be reversed.

Here are some successful breakout session ideas we have used over the years:

- Provide information about the CCSS for parents, such as a discussion about reading informational text and how to use it at home.
- Model different elements of language arts that are more interactive or playful, such as drama. Show parents they can gather simple dress-up items and create oral stories. Even older students enjoy this activity.
- Construct areas for making and looking at children's literature. Parents may not know how to make books with children, so show families how to use common materials, such as paper, cardstock, markers, stickers, and crayons to make different types of books. Making family books is enjoyable but also gives families something to take home that can be read over and over again. Making a bookmark is a simpler adaptation.
- Collect and play board and electronic games. Have teachers and students bring in their favorite games, and show off the ones that use critical-thinking strategies.

Putting It All Together: One School's Story

By now you must be wondering how a school puts all the pieces together. What we know for sure is that each school will develop its own path that works best for the learning community. Schools have unique cultures and personalities that will enter into and shape the process. The question of time is often considered, both in terms of how long it will take to become a new balanced literacy school and how school communities will find the time to accomplish all of these tasks. We know that this process takes weeks, months, and even years to fulfill. One principal at a model school said it took 10 years to develop all of the in-school libraries. We encourage you to start with one library and then add a library at a time. Celebrate the small changes as they occur, and keep your eye on the target: providing access to books for student learning.

We recently worked with one school and, within a few months, we saw measurable progress in many areas, both physical and organizational. This school had a kick-off workshop for balanced literacy the last week of school before summer vacation. We were certainly hesitant about how that would be received by the teachers. In addition, students were sent home for the summer with readings on balanced literacy. Immediately, the principal formed a school-wide literacy team that met over the summer to roll out a plan for the start of school. During this time over the summer, they recruited parent volunteers to help design and create the parent library. They had a second workshop on balanced literacy for their back-to-school professional development. An information session on balanced literacy was planned and presented to the parents before school started so that the parent community would be fully informed about the changes that were happening school wide with instruction. The energy within the school began to change, and everyone got excited about the movement toward balanced literacy. One teacher remarked that she felt "like a first-year teacher all over again." We loved watching this process unfold. The key element here was that the principal utilized the summer as an action-oriented planning period to get things moving. In September, the principal set important deadlines for things to be accomplished by. For example, a date of October 1 was given for all teachers to have word walls up in their classrooms and read-alouds posted outside their classroom doors. Physical classroom structures had to change to create an environment that fostered student collaboration and cooperation. In just 18 months, this school transformed physically and increased school-wide capacity building through teams and collaboration. The following timeline shows what this school did in a matter of months to begin to bring about school-wide change.

At-a-Glance: The First 18 Months of Setting up a New Balanced Literacy School

May	Professional development workshop on balanced literacy
June	Formation of a school-wide literacy team
June–August	• Teachers read materials about balanced literacy over the summer • Literacy team met and began planning for rolling out balanced literacy and forming a school-wide mission statement on literacy • Parent volunteers were recruited to assist with parent library • Back-to-school professional development for teachers planned • Information session for parents planned and implemented
August–September	• Deadlines established by the principal for certain aspects of balanced literacy to begin • Entryway begins transformation for parent library • Teachers get more training on guided reading and assessments
October	• Teachers had read-alouds posted outside their classroom doors • Word walls posted in classrooms • Classrooms arranged to support and facilitate small-group instruction • Common Core exemplar text library set placed in balanced literacy library
November–January	• Self-assessment and reflection inventories on balanced literacy • Began filling out the 110 Minutes of Daily Balanced Literacy routines • Professional development on guiding reading and benchmark assessments

February–March	• Balanced literacy team furthered the school-wide goals to incorporate word walls into lessons along with the purpose for read-alouds • Teachers took classroom walk-throughs to share their word walls • Professional development in the CCSS instructional shifts
April–June	• School-wide book club on professional learning communities • Literacy team devised grade-level meeting protocols and forms • Summer reading assigned for teachers • Professional development on close reading and other shifts
June–August	• Summer reading initiative (SRI) • Professional development workshops
September–November	• Word walls move into language walls • Writing workshop PK–8 is rolled out • Grade-level meetings focus on student learning and follow the PLC protocol

What Have We Learned? Lessons from the Schools

Over all these years, we have learned many lessons about working to create balanced literacy schools. The first and most difficult lesson is that there will always be setbacks. Setbacks are a natural part of life. Setbacks in schools can be anything from a small transition in administration and resistance from teachers to teacher turnover and school closings. We are always optimistic about the quest that we are on track, but we are also realistic and realize things happen that we have no control over. Despite challenges that arise, we have learned to keep going and persevere. What else have we learned?

- We have learned that principals really want the best for their schools.
- We have learned that resistance does not mean you can't move forward.
- We have learned that, despite teacher turnover, bringing new teachers on board will work.
- We have learned that so many teachers are excited about balanced literacy, ongoing professional development, and embracing their new learning.
- We have learned to never give up—no matter where a school is at in its quest toward balanced literacy—because there is no ending point.
- We have learned that balanced literacy is a continuous process.
- We have learned that the field of literacy is always in a stage of renewal, and schools must be ready for what research presents as the next best practice.
- We have learned that when you provide a little bit of professional development to teachers, they want to learn more.
- We have learned that a new school-wide coaching model is necessary as it positions coaches to build capacity within literacy and grade-level teams.
- We have learned that there is no magic bullet or quick fix and that this is a long-term process requiring school-wide buy-in and collaboration.

References

Allington, R.L. & McGill-Franzen, A. (Eds.). (2013). (Eds.) *Summer reading: Closing the rich/poor reading achievement gap.* New York, NY: Teachers College Press.

Asselin, M. (1999). Balanced literacy. *Teacher Librarian,* 27(1), 69–70.

Bean, R. M. (2009). *The reading specialist: leadership for the classroom, school, and community* (2nd ed.). New York, NY: Guilford Press.

Beck, I. L., McKeown, M. G., & Kucan, L. (2002). *Bringing words to life: Robust vocabulary instruction.* New York, NY: Guilford Press.

Blachowicz, C. Z., & Ogle, D. (2001). *Reading comprehension: Strategies for independent learners.* New York, NY: Guilford Press.

Blachowicz, C. Z., Buhle, R., Ogle, D., Frost, S., Correa, A., & Kinner, J. (2010). Hit the ground running: Ten ideas for preparing and supporting urban literacy coaches. *Reading Teacher,* 63(5), 348–359.

Booth, D., & Rowsell., J. (2007). *The literacy principal: Leading, supporting, and assessing reading and writing initiatives* (2nd ed.). Markham, Ont.: Pembroke Publishers.

Brown, J. (1964). *Flat Stanley.* New York, NY: Harper & Row.

Brown, M.W. (1947). *Goodnight moon.* New York, NY: Harper.

California Department of Education (1996). *Teaching reading: A balanced comprehensive approach to teaching reading in prekindergarten through grade three.* Sacramento, CA: Authors.

Cassidy, J., Garrett, S., Maxfield, P., & Patchett, C. (2009). *Literacy coaching: Yesterday, today and tomorrow. CEDER Yearbook,* 15–27.

Chang, M. L. (2004). *Classroom management in photographs: Full-color photographs with teacher descriptions and insights about what really works.* New York, NY: Scholastic.

Clay, M. M. (2001). *Change over time in children's literacy development.* Portsmouth, NH: Heinemann.

Cobb, C. (2005). Speaking to administrators and reading specialists literacy teams: Sharing leadership to improve student learning. *Reading Teacher,* 58(5), 472–474.

Cohen, V. L., & Cowen, J. E. (2011). *Literacy for children in an information age: Teaching reading, writing, and thinking* (2nd ed.). Belmont, CA: Wadsworth, Cengage Learning.

Cummins, J. (1999). BICS and CALP: Clarifying the distinction. *University of Toronto, Opinion Papers* (120).

Darling-Hammond, L. (2010). *The flat world and education: How America's commitment to equity will determine our future.* New York, NY: Teachers College Press.

Diffily, D., & Sassman, C. (2004). *Teaching effective classroom routines: Establish structure in the classroom to foster children's learning, from the first day of school and all through the year.* New York, NY: Scholastic.

Diller, D. (2003). *Literacy work stations: Making centers work.* Portland, ME: Stenhouse.

Duncan, A. (October 24, 2013). *Implementing the Common Core.* Institute of Politics lecture, University of Chicago.

Eaker, R., DuFour, R.; & DuFour, R. (2002). *Getting started: Reculturing schools to become professional learning communities.* Bloomington, IN: Solution Trees.

Eilers, L. H., & D'Amico, M. (2012). Essential leadership elements in implementing common core state standards. *Delta Kappa Gamma Bulletin,* 78(4), 46–50.

Falk-Ross, F. (2011). Helping literacy centers come alive for teachers: Transitions into use of interactive small group reading stations. *College Reading Association Yearbook.* Issue 29, 237–247.

Ferguson, J., & Wilson, J., (2009). Guided reading: It's for primary teachers. *College Reading Association Yearbook.* Issue 30, 293–306.

Fisher, B., & Medvic, E. F. (2000). *Perspectives on shared reading: Planning and practice.* Portsmouth, NH: Heinemann.

Fisher, D., & Frey, N. (2012). Close reading in elementary schools. *The Reading Teacher,* 66(3), 179.

Fisher, D., & Frey, N. (2012). Literacy achievement through sustained professional development. *The Reading Teacher,* 65(8), 551–563.

Fitzgerald, J. (1999). What is this thing called "balance"? *The Reading Teacher,* 53(2), 100–107.

Fountas, I. C. & Pinnell, G. S. (1996). *Guided reading: Good first teaching for all children.* Portsmouth, NH: Heinemann.

Fountas, I. C. & Pinnell, G. S. (1999). *Guiding readers and writers, grades 3–6: Teaching comprehension, genre, and content literacy.* Portsmouth, NH: Heinemann.

Fountas, I. C. & Pinnell, G. S. (2012). Guided reading: The romance and the reality. *The Reading Teacher,* 66(4), 268.

French, C., Morgan, J., Vanayan, M., & White, N. (2001). Balanced literacy: Implementation and evaluation. *Education Canada,* 40(4), 23.

Freppon, P. A., & Dahl, K. L. (1998). Balanced instruction: Insights and considerations. *Reading Research Quarterly,* 33(2), 240.

Frey, B. B., Lee, S. W., Tollefson, N., Pass, L., & Massengill, D. (2005). Balanced literacy in an urban school district. *Journal of Educational Research,* 98(5), 272–280.

Fullan, M. (2007). *The new meaning of educational change* (4th ed.). New York, NY: Teachers College Press.

Fullan, M. & Quinn, J. (2012). Leading transformational change in a changing world. Retrieved October 2013 from http://www.michaelfullan.ca/images/handouts/12_ISTE_Opening%28V03%29.pdf.

Gambrell, L. B. (2011). Seven rules of engagement: What's most important to know about motivation to read. *Reading Teacher,* 65(3), 172–178.

Gee, J. (2001). Reading as situated language: A sociocognitive perspective. *Journal of Adolescent & Adult Literacy,* 44(8), 714.

Gewertz, C. (2012). Common standards drive new reading approaches. *Education Week,* 32(12), S2.

Goodman, K. S. (1969). Analysis of oral reading miscues: Applied psycholinguistics. *Reading Research Quarterly,* 5, 9–30.

Goodman, K. S. (1996). *On reading.* Portsmouth, NH: Heinemann.

Halliday, M.A.K. (1993). Towards a language-based theory of learning. *Linguistics and Education,* 5, 93–116.

Hancock, M. R. (2007). *Language arts: Extending the possibilities.* Upper Saddle River, NJ: Pearson Merrill Prentice Hall.

Hargraves, A. & Fullan, M. (2012) *Professional capital: Transforming teaching in every school.* New York, NY: Teachers College Press.

Harris, V. J. (2012). On creating a diverse classroom library. *Journal of Children's Literature,* 38(1), 75–76.

Honig, W. (1996). *Teaching our children to read: The role of skills in a comprehensive reading program.* Thousand Oaks, CA: Corwin Press.

Huffman, J. & Hipp, K. (2003). *Reculturing schools as professional learning communities.* Lanham, MD: Scarecrow Education.

International Reading Association Common Core State Standards (CCSS) Committee. (2012). *Literacy implementation guidance for the ELA Common Core State Standards* [White paper].

Johnston, P. (2004). *Choice Words.* Portland, OR: Stenhouse.

Jones, J.A. (2006). Student-involved classroom libraries. *The Reading Teacher,* 59(6). 576–580.

Langer, J. (2004). *Getting to excellent: How to create better schools.* New York, NY: Teachers College Press.

Lieberman, A. (2000). Learning Communities: Shaping the future of teacher development. *Journal of Teacher Education,* 51: 221–227.

Lindsay, J. (2013). Interventions that increase children's access to print material and improve their reading proficiencies. In R. L. Allington & A. McGill-Franzen (Eds.), *Summer reading: Closing the rich/poor reading achievement gap.* (pp. 20–38). New York, NY: Teachers College Press.

Lyman, F. T. (1981). The responsive classroom discussion: The inclusion of all students. In A. Anderson (Ed.), *Mainstreaming Digest.* (pp. 109–113). College Park, MD: University of Maryland Press.

Madda, C. L., Griffo, V.B.; Pearson, P.D. & Raphael, T.E. (2007.) Balance in comprehensive literacy instruction. In L. M. Morrow & L. B. Gambrell (Eds.), *Best practices in literacy instruction,* 4th ed. (pp. 37–67). New York, NY: Guilford Press.

Massey, S. (2012/13). Leadership roles in implementing the common core state standards. *Illinois Reading Council Journal,* 41(1), 67.

Mermelstein, L. (n.d.). The components of balanced literacy. *Education.com.* Retrieved September 3, 2013, from http://www.education.com/reference/article/components-balanced-literacy.

Nace, F. (2013). Building a professional development library: Five time-saving strategies to maximize your PD resources and bolster your staff's learning. *Principal* (January/February 2013). Retrieved November 2013 from http://www.naesp.org/principal-janfeb-2013-teacher-staff-development/building-professional-development-library.

National Governors Association Center for Best Practices & Council of Chief State School Officers. (2010). *Common Core State Standards.* Washington, DC: Authors.

National Governors Association Center for Best Practices & Council of Chief State School Officers. Frequently asked questions. In *Common Core State Standards.* Retrieved November 19, 2013, from http://www.corestandards.org/assets/CoreFAQ.pdf.

National Governors Association Center for Best Practices & Council of Chief State School Officers. Mission statement. In *Common Core State Standards.* Retrieved November 5, 2013, from http://www.corestandards.org.

Nelson, Catherine A., Robert Hill, Michael Palmisano, Lara Hebert, and Sharon Roth. The NCLE Framework for Capacity Building. Urbana, IL: *National Center for Literacy Education,* 2012. Retrieved August 2013. http://www.literacyinlearningexchange.org/sites/default/files/capacitybuildingframework_0.pdf

O'Day, J., Goertz, M. E., & Floden, R. E. (1995). Building capacity for education reform. *CPRE Policy Briefs.*

Opitz, M. F. & Ford, M. P. (2001). *Reaching readers: Flexible & innovative strategies for guided reading.* Portsmouth, NH: Heinemann.

Partnership for Assessment of Readiness for College and Careers | PARCC. (n.d.). *Partnership for assessment of readiness for college and careers* | PARCC. Retrieved November 19, 2013, from http://www.parcconline.org.

Policastro, M. M. (2008). The bedtime story. *Reach Out and Read Newsletter of the American Academy of Pediatrics.*

Policastro, M. M., Mazeski, D. K., & McTague, B. (2010). Parent involvement in reading. *Illinois Reading Council Journal,* 39(1), 60–64.

Rudell, R. B., & Unrau, N. J. (2004). Reading as a motivated meaning-constructed process: The reader, the text and the teacher. In Alvermann, D. E., R. B. Rudell, & N. J. Unrau (Eds.), *Theoretical models and processes of reading* (5th ed.) (pp. 1462–1521). Newark. DE: International Reading Association.

Rudell, R. B., Rudell, M. R., & Singer, H. (Eds.) (1994). *Theoretical models and processes of reading.* (4th ed). Newark, DE: International Reading Association.

Sanden, S. (2012). Independent reading: Perspectives and practices of highly effective teachers. *Reading Teacher,* 66(3), 222–231.

Serafini, F. (2011). Creating space for children's literature. *Reading Teacher,* 65(1), 30–34.

Shanahan, T. (2013, October 17). Common visions, common goals: Preparing schools, colleges and universities for the new standards and assessments. *Common Visions, Common Goals.* Lecture conducted from Bone Student Center, Center for the Study of Education Policy, Illinois State University, Normal, IL.

Shea, M., Murray, R., & Harlin, R. (2005). *Drowning in data? How to collect and document student performance.* Portsmouth, NH: Heinemann.

Smarter Balanced Assessment Consortium. (n.d.). *Smarter Balanced Assessment Consortium.* Retrieved November 19, 2013, from http://www.smarterbalanced.org.

Smith, F. (2004). *Understanding reading: A psycholinguistic analysis of reading and learning to read.* Mahwah, NJ: L. Erlbaum and Associates.

Spiegel, D. (1998). Silver bullets, babies, and bath water: Literature response groups in a balanced literacy program. *Reading Teacher,* 52(2), 114.

Stout, R. (2009). Putting literacy centers to work: A novice teacher utilizes literacy centers to improve reading instruction. *Networks: An Online Journal for Teacher Research,* 11(1), 1–6.

Taylor, R. T. & Gunter, G. A. (2006). *The K–12 literacy leadership field book.* Thousand Oaks, CA: Corwin Press.

The National Center for Literacy Education (n.d.). *NCTE Comprehensive News.* Retrieved August 2013 from http://www.ncte.org/ncle.

Tompkins, G. E. (2010, 2013). *Literacy for the 21st century: A balanced approach* (5th ed.). Upper Saddle River, NJ: Pearson.

Tracy, D. H. & Morrow, L. M. (2006). *Lenses on reading: An introduction to theories and models.* NY: Guilford Press.

Unrau, N. J. & Alvermann ,D. E. (2013). Literacies and their investigation through theories and models. In Alvermann, D. E., R. B. Rudell, & N. J. Unrau (Eds.), *Theoretical models and processes of reading,* 5th ed. (pp. 47–90). Newark, DE: International Reading Association.

Vygotsky, L. (1986). *Thought and language.* Cambridge, MA: MIT Press.

Welcome To Achieve | Achieve. (n.d.). *Welcome To Achieve | Achieve.* Retrieved November 19, 2013, from http://achieve.org.

Wick, W. (1997). *A drop of water: A book of science and wonder.* New York, NY: Scholastic Press.

Appendices

Appendix A: An Organizational Framework for Multiple In-School Libraries

An organizational framework for multiple in-school libraries: parent library, read-aloud library, guided reading library, novel sets library, classroom library, professional development library, and the school hallbrary.

Access to Books: Parents, Teachers and Administrators, and Children

Access to books involves including the parents, teachers and administrators, and children.

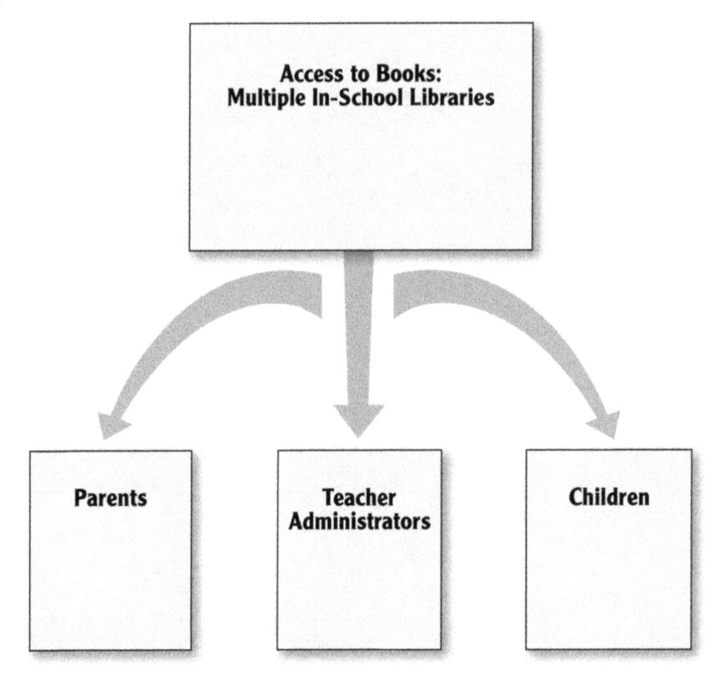

Beyond providing access to books, there is a process that takes place in developing libraries. The three key library elements of access, management, and collection overlap in structure due to the nature of libraries. For example, when planning where a library will be located, it is important to consider the size of the collection and how books will circulate. When considering who will be using the library, it is important to take into account how easy it is to access the location. The time of day and hours for usage are essential to consider as well when serving all the possible school audiences.

Key Library Elements: Access, Collection, and Management

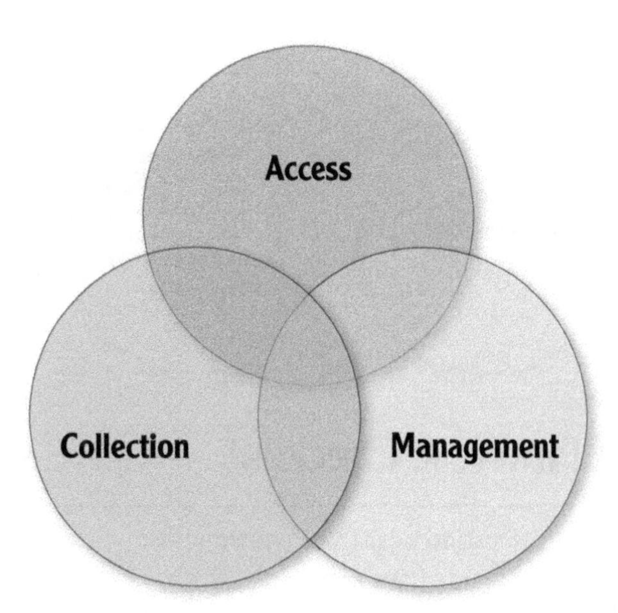

- **ACCESS** includes where the library might be located within a school to be inviting. This could be in a hallway, near the front entrance, in a classroom, etc. The ease with which books can be accessed must be considered.

- **COLLECTION** consists of the range and variety of genres (Common Core exemplars, fiction, nonfiction), along with the quantity and quality of books. How new editions are selected and added is key.

- **MANAGEMENT** focuses on how books circulate for the users. Ordering of new books along with the visual display and arrangement are also key elements.

The Parent Library

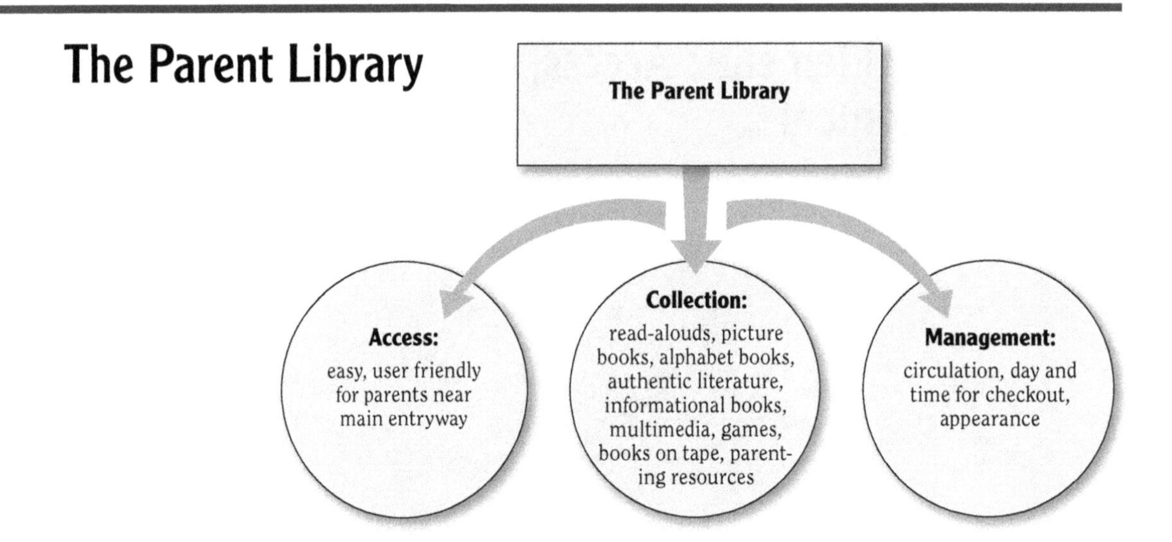

The Parent Library: A Checklist

Access	___ location near front entryway ___ parents have easy access ___ inviting to the parent community ___ places to sit and read (bench, cozy chairs)
Collection	___ dual-language books that consider language of users ___ read-aloud books ___ bedtime story selections ___ picture books ___ alphabet books and concept books ___ authentic literature ___ books for infants and toddlers ___ classic and contemporary books ___ informational texts ___ books on tape ___ educational games ___ children's magazines ___ books and information on parenting ___ handouts on reading aloud to your child ___ "Six Tips for Reading Aloud" (page 44) ___ reading lists on best read-aloud books ___ suggestion box near the collection
Management	___ keep a checkout system in place ___ stand up books for inviting displays ___ post times for checkout ___ label the categories of available books ___ upkeep the library ___ order new books and materials

The Read-Aloud Library

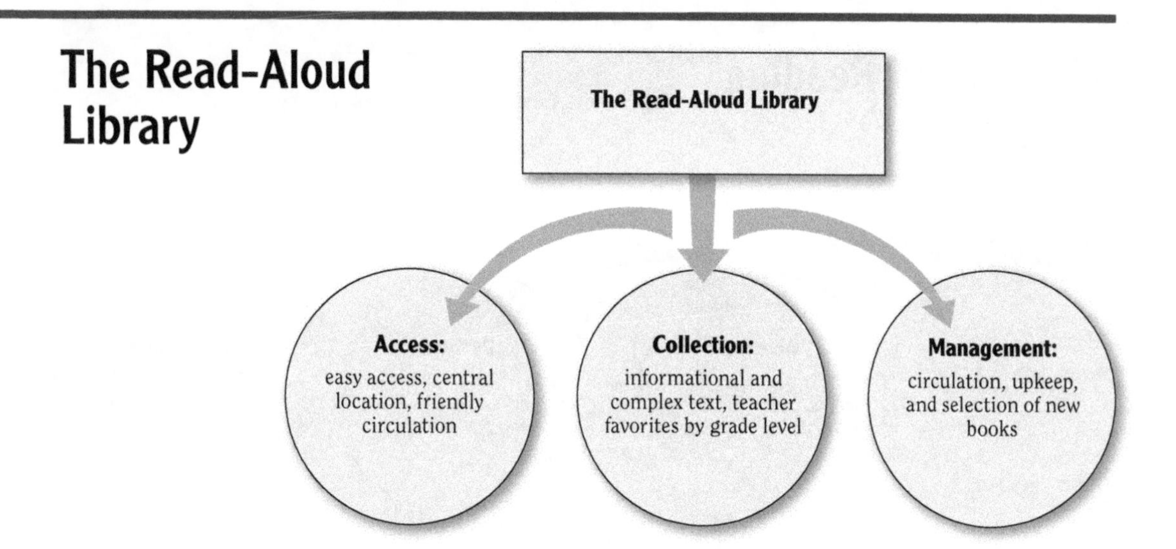

The Read-Aloud Library: A Checklist

Access	___ located where all teachers have easy access ___ a central location (lounge, hallway) ___ circulation should be friendly and easy
Collection	___ teacher favorites by grade level ___ shared agreement of books ___ exemplar texts from CCSS Appendix B ___ award-winning books ___ 50% informational text and complex texts ___ interactive and pop-out books ___ books for all grade levels ___ poetry, biographies ___ read-aloud book lists ___ "Six Tips for Reading Aloud" (page 44) ___ suggestion box near the collection
Management	___ make available during all school hours ___ keep a checkout system in place ___ stand up books for inviting displays ___ upkeep the collection ___ label and identify the categories of books ___ order new books ___ rotate books from the school library

The Guided Reading Library

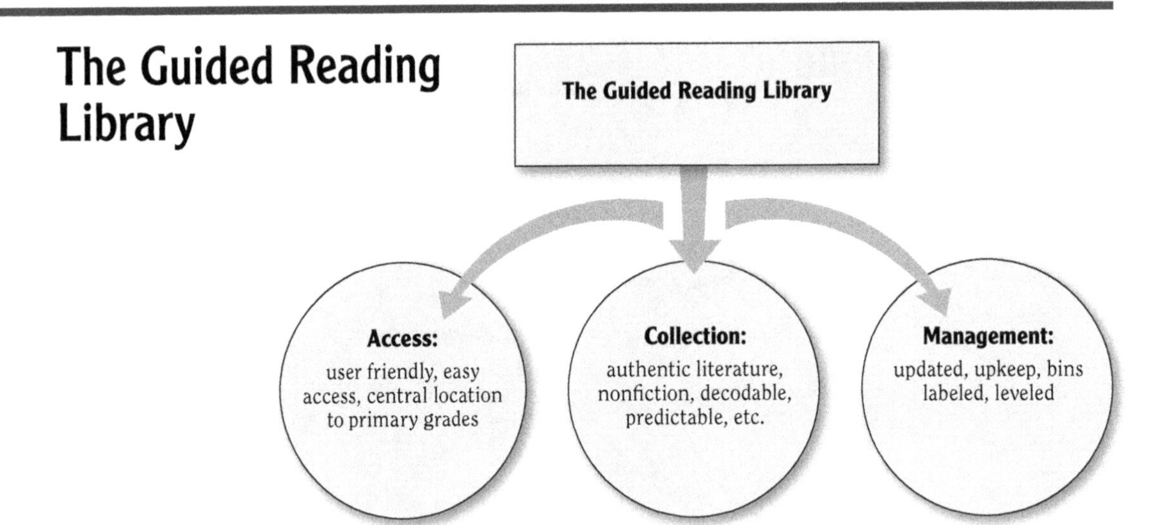

The Guided Reading Library: A Checklist

Access	___located in a central location (primary and intermediate grades) ___user-friendly circulation
Collection	___authentic literature ___fiction, nonfiction, and informational texts ___wide range and variety of books ___decodable and predictable books ___books leveled according to the new text complexity ___books labeled with levels ___books in bins for easy transporting
Management	___keep library open during all school hours ___have a user-friendly checkout system ___upkeep the materials ___update and order new materials

The Novel Sets Library

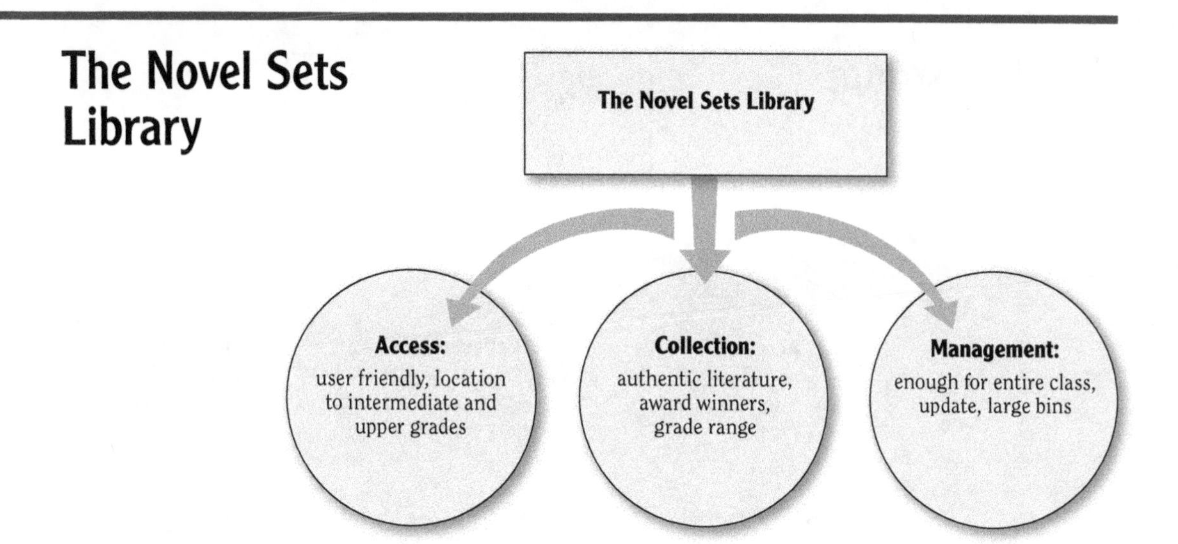

The Novel Sets Library: A Checklist

Access	___located near the intermediate and upper grades ___user-friendly access and checkout system ___open during all school hours
Collection	___teacher favorites by grade level ___shared agreements by teachers ___award-winning books ___exemplar texts from CCSS Appendix B ___informational texts ___keep a suggestion box near the collection
Management	___keep a checkout system in place ___use bins for class sets ___label by grade range and title ___consider text complexity and CCSS with level ___order new books

The Classroom Library

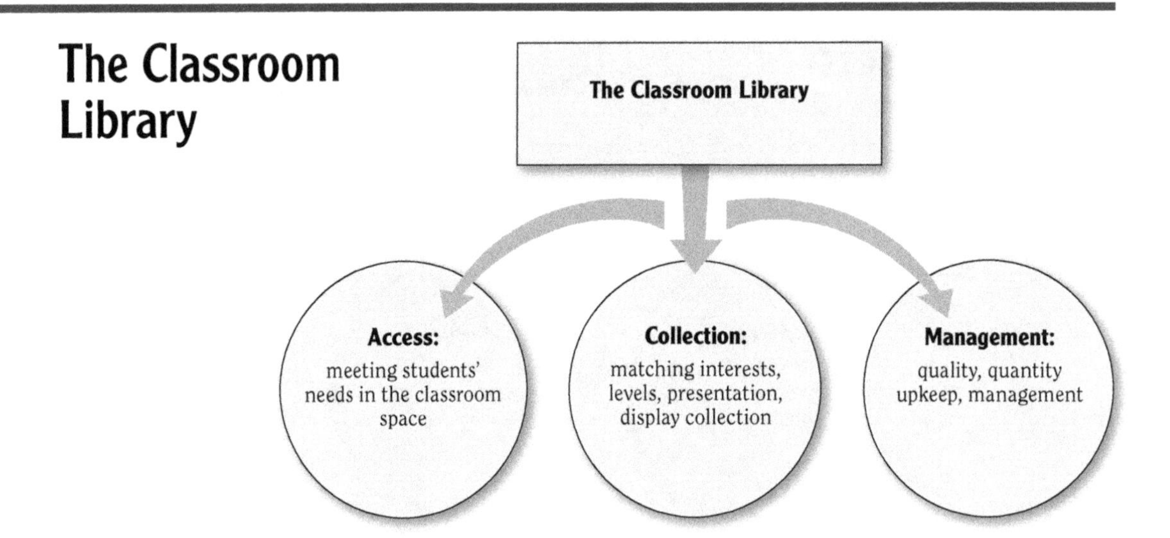

The Classroom Library: A Checklist

Access	___ located in the classroom for easy access ___ considers the movement of students ___ considers the height of the collection ___ a cozy space for independent reading
Collection	___ wide range and variety of books to meet interests and needs ___ at least 50% informational text in all content areas ___ challenging texts ___ books that entertain ___ magazines ___ award-winning books ___ exemplar texts from CCSS Appendix B ___ poetry, graphic novels, humorous books ___ books for after school and home reading ___ a suggestion box near the collection
Management	___ keep a checkout system in place ___ stand up books for inviting displays ___ label books and bins by topic, genre, and a range of levels ___ have students take responsibility for upkeep

The Professional Development Library

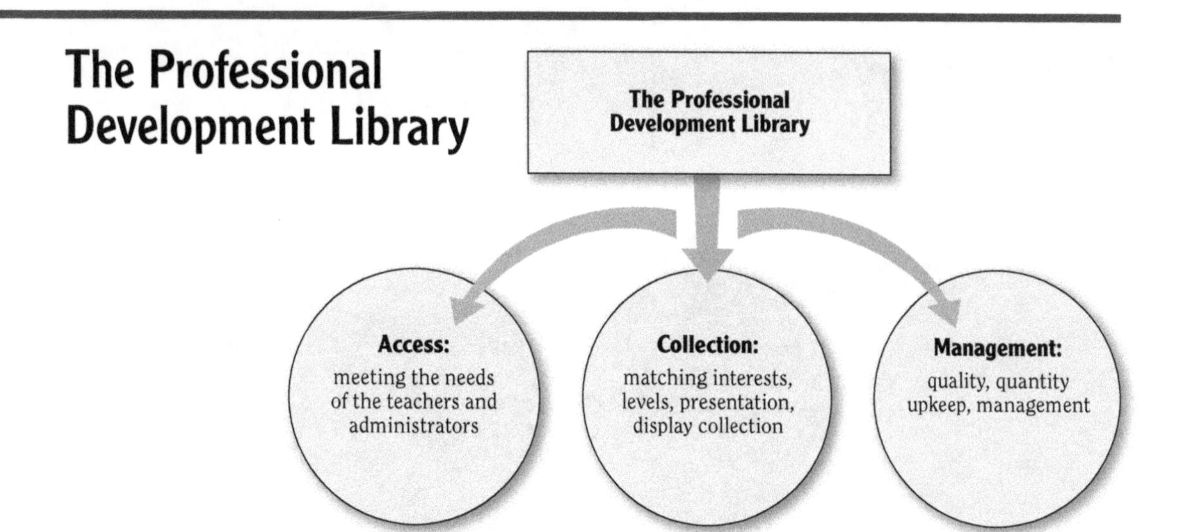

The Professional Development Library: A Checklist

Access	___ located where teachers meet or gather ___ easy access ___ user-friendly checkout system ___ available during all school hours ___ inviting space for teachers to browse, read, and discuss readings
Collection	___ wide range of books on best practices in literacy and pedagogy ___ multiple copies of books ___ classics in the field (Kozol, Bloom) ___ specific books on implementing the CCSS ___ short articles on tips or strategies for teaching ___ articles for conversations and discussions in team meetings ___ books on professional learning communities ___ books on teaching strategies ___ professional journals (*The Reading Teacher*) ___ videos of best practices and strategies ___ suggestion box near the collection
Management	___ keep current with best practices ___ have a checkout system in place ___ label the collection by topic

The Hallbrary

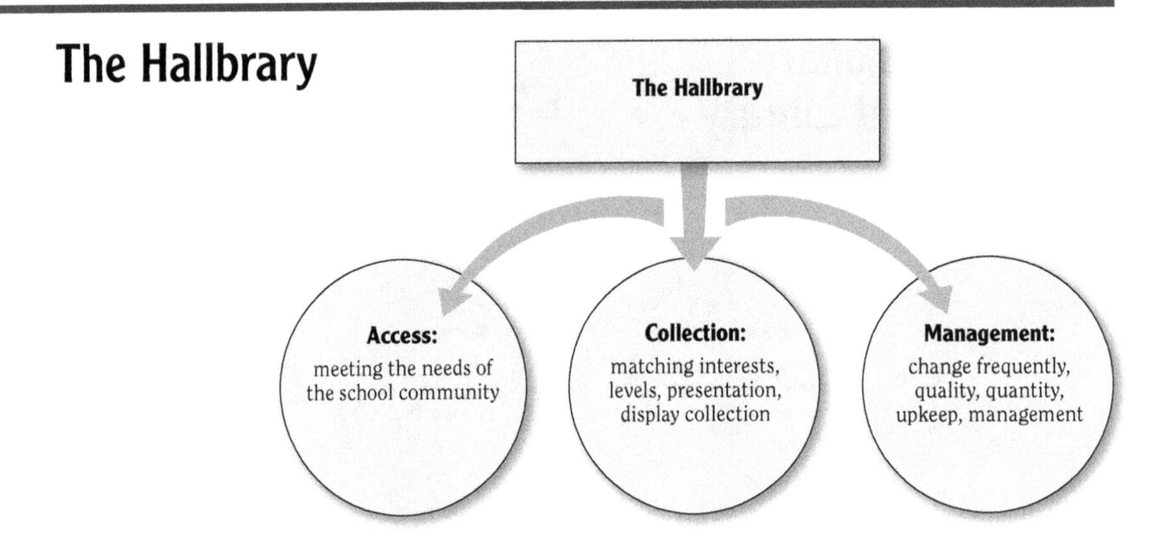

The Hallbrary: A Checklist

Access	___located in a corner space or near a window ___considers movement around the space during school hours ___rocking chair and carpet to make it an inviting place
Collection	___new titles and books ___award winners ___back-to-school reading ___summer reading book suggestions ___holidays and celebration books ___books from "The Read-Aloud Library" checklist (page 119)
Management	___do not allow books to be checked out of the hallbrary ___change the collection frequently

Appendix B: A Guide to Creating a New Balanced Literacy School

This process of creating a new balanced literacy school can take many months and years to complete. It is a not a linear process but rather a continuous process. We suggest that you use this book and the following information as a guide. School teams will decide where to begin as it is a rather large endeavor and can be overwhelming.

Guiding Principle: Create a Literacy Team

- Begin with the establishment of a school-wide literacy team and seek out volunteers to join.
- Meet on a weekly basis for the first year.
- Establish an agenda and protocol for meetings.
- Establish a school-wide mission and vision statement for what literacy will look like in the school.
- Plan a session for parents to introduce the community to balanced literacy.
- Begin to establish a timeline with exact dates to roll out the tenets of balanced literacy that include the 110 Minutes of Daily Balanced Literacy routine in each classroom.
- Begin to establish rollout dates for the individual tenets of balanced literacy: read-alouds, language and literacy centers, guided reading, word walls to language wall, independent reading and writing, and classroom libraries.
- Establish a timeline for ongoing and systematic professional development that includes workshops, book clubs, and other professional readings.

Guiding Principle: Develop Multiple In-School Libraries

- Begin an inventory of all the books within the school, including guided reading sets and multiple copies of books and novel sets that may be in classrooms.
- For the parent library, begin to think of a space near the entryway that would be inviting to parents.
- Begin to think of a room for the guided reading, read-aloud, and novel sets collections. This room serves as a central location for all the balanced literacy materials and resources.
- Take an inventory of the bookshelves and other materials, such as bins and baskets that will be needed to build the libraries.

Guiding Principle: Establish High-Functioning Grade-Level Teams

- Develop a schedule for when grade-level teams will meet on a weekly basis.
- Develop an agenda and protocol template for the grade-level meetings.
- Focus the meetings on analyzing student data and learning.

Guiding Principle: Become a Professional Learning Community

- Make the choice to build capacity through collaborative professional learning communities.
- Start a school-wide book club.
- Focus on student learning as the main priority for all teams.

Appendix C: Summer Reading Initiatives (SRI)

Sample Summer Reading Initiatives (SRI) in a New Balanced Literacy School

Listed below are some examples of summer reading initiatives that have been tried in the schools we work with. Each example is different since there is no one way to launch a summer reading program. The key here is to provide access to books for children during the summer months.

Christ the King School; Chicago, Illinois

This school decided to launch their summer reading initiative after their Sunday church services. This worked well as it invited the entire community to take part. Tables and displays were set up outside the church, and teachers volunteered to help the children check out books. This took place over the summer months, and the children who participated were treated to a pizza party before school started. Here is their flier.

Got Books?

Christ the King (CK) has been very busy these last few months working with Roosevelt University in developing a school-wide balanced literacy program. CK, in conjunction with Roosevelt, has launched a summer reading initiative all summer!

Balanced literacy incorporates all the components of language arts—reading, writing, speaking, listening, and vocabulary. Beyond that, balanced literacy is necessary across the curriculum—science, social studies, math, music, art, and any other subjects being taught. These components are linked to the Common Core Standards the state of Illinois has adopted.

CK has been ahead of the game in already incorporating those standards based on the resources and assessment guidelines already present. Our teachers have been attending workshops, reading books, and digging up resources online to incorporate into their lesson plans.

It is a fact that there is what is referred to as "summer reading loss" that takes teachers a couple of weeks of the new school year to catch the students up to where they were at the end of the previous school year. We can help.

You do not have to be a student of CK. Every Sunday from 9:00 a.m. to 12:30 p.m., teachers and volunteers will be available in the vestibule of the church with books, books, and more books. Just stop by and browse through a collection of books that are grouped by grade level. You are welcome to find that special book, take it home, and keep it—no charge!

The only thing you would need to do is register and complete a reading log.

At the end of the program, CK will be hosting a celebration at the school and your only entry ticket is to bring your log and join the party!

See you Sunday!

Christ the King School Summer Reading Initiative: Church Announcement (Target audience: all children at mass)

Christ the King School is excited to announce the kick-off to our "Summer Reading Initiative." This program is supported through a Balanced Literacy Grant, which Christ the King received through its partnership with Roosevelt University. The purpose of this initiative is to promote reading throughout the summer months. After each Mass on Sunday (8:00, 9:30, and 11:00 a.m.) beginning June 16 and running through August 4, all children entering grades kindergarten through ninth will be able to take home a summer reading selection of their choice. Younger children, who may be non-readers, can still participate if someone is willing to read a book to them.

These books will be available outside the front doors of church, weather permitting, and inside the church vestibule when the weather is inclement. Children may keep this book at no charge; however, we ask that they complete a reading log for each book read. Once students have completed reading their book, they are free to stop by and choose another book of their choice while supplies last.

All students who submit one or more reading logs by August 11 are invited to attend our end-of-the-program celebration. More details will be provided in August. Please know children who are visitors to Christ the King are welcome to choose a book as well. Our goal is to get these books into our young learners' hands so they keep reading throughout the summer. We have many wonderful books just waiting to be read by your children. Please stop after mass and support this important initiative. We look forward to seeing you after the Sunday masses.

Also, we are in need of parent and junior high student volunteers to help "man" the cart before, during, and after the masses. Students entering grade seven and eight can earn service hours for their help. The time slots are Sundays, 8:45–10:00 a.m., 10:00–11:15 a.m., and 11:15 a.m.–12:45 p.m. We would need at least one adult volunteer for each time slot. The first time slot would require set-up, and the last time slot would require storing the materials. The books will be on a cart to make set-up and clean-up an easy task. If you are available to help, please contact the school office.

Summer Reading Initiative Celebration

The Balanced Literacy Leadership Team would like to thank all the children that participated in the Summer Reading Initiative supported through the Balanced Literacy Grant provided by Roosevelt University. We would like to celebrate the end of this program with a pizza party on Thursday, August 15. If your family filled out a registration form with an e-mail address, then you will be receiving an e-vite within the next few days. If you do not receive the e-vite, please know all participants in our Summer Reading Initiative are welcome to attend.

Summer Reading Initiative Wrap-Up Party

Thursday, August 15, 12:00–1:00 p.m.

Parish Center Rooms 2/3. Please enter through the Parish Center north doors on Hoyne. For our children's safety, all participants must be picked up and signed out by an adult (18 or over). Students must bring all of their completed reading logs.

We will serve individual cheese pizzas.

Our Lady of the Wayside School; Arlington Heights, Illinois

This school decided to have the summer books available to the students on Wednesdays during the summer. The books were displayed near the entryway of the building. The schedule alternated between mornings and afternoons to accommodate everyone. Teachers volunteered in assisting with the check-out of the books. They paired up with a local yogurt store and the children who completed the summer reading initiative were given a coupon for a free yogurt.

Perkins Bass School; Chicago, Illinois

This school decided to have books readily available on Saturday mornings during the summer. The books were distributed near the entryway of the school and teachers volunteered to check out the books for the students.

Appendix D: Balanced Literacy Umbrella Template

Appendix E: Professional Development

This section is designed to offer ideas for principals and school leaders about ongoing professional development. The first section lists topics and questions for conversation and discussion within grade-level and literacy team meetings. These points are meant to be reflective and facilitate learning. The second section lists potential workshop topics.

Discussion Points for Grade-Level and Literacy Team Meetings

- Where are we as a new balanced literacy school? What steps do we need to take to become a new balanced literacy school?
- Where are we with access to books year-round, including for summer, children, parents, teachers, and administrators?
- What does our student assessment data look like for each grade and as a school?
- How can we become a professional learning community? What steps do we need to take?
- How can we make sure that the focus of our school is on student learning? What would that look like in all classrooms?
- How can we build capacity as a professional learning community? How can we share our practices? How can we share agreements about students and decision making?
- What does our home-school partnership look like? How can we bring parents into our community? What special events can we have to promote family literacy throughout the entire year, including summer?
- What topics of interest could we develop to offer parent workshops? How can we encourage parents to volunteer in the school?

Professional Development Workshop Topics: Two-Year Plan

Year One

- What is balanced literacy? Introduction to the organizational and structural tenets
- What does a balanced literacy school Look like? Multiple in-school libraries
- What does a balanced literacy school look like with CCSS?
- What does the new read-aloud look like in a balanced literacy classroom?
- What is guided reading? How to guide language into reading
- What is a language and literacy center?
- Moving from word walls to language walls
- What is a professional learning community (PLC)?

Year Two

- What does capacity building look like in a balanced literacy school?
- Creating the literate environment: What does the balanced literacy classroom look like?
- Set up the literacy routine: 110 Minutes of Daily Balanced Literacy.
- How do we set up units of study that reflect CCSS?
- What does assessment look like in a balanced literacy classroom?
- How do assessment and instruction merge in a balanced literacy classroom?
- What does close reading look like in a balanced literacy classroom?

Appendix F: My Close Reading Kit

In response to the need to shift instructional strategies to highlight close reading, we have developed a close reading kit for teachers. This kit grew out of the concern about how to document students' close reading. This is meant to be an active tool that students use during many reading lessons and activities, such as:

- Guiding language into reading
- Language and literacy centers
- Independent reading and writing

Our intention was to develop a working documentation so students could keep account of their close reading. This is a metacognitive task as students are becoming aware of their close reading skills. In the close reading kit, we have included: bendable craft sticks, which can be used by teachers and students to highlight words and sentences as they close read; My Close Reading Account sheets (by primary, intermediate, and upper grades); and colored highlighting tape for highlighting words, phrases, and evidence. We also include a small magnifying glass to remind students that this is a different kind of reading that requires close-up investigation of the text. The pages that follow include templates of the My Close Reading Account Sheets.

My Close Reading Account: Primary

Name: ______________________ Date: ______

Title: ______________________________

Author: ______________________________

What is my purpose for reading?

____

____

____

3-2-1-1 Strategy

3 things I learned

2 interesting details

1 question

1 what's important?

What did I learn? (cite evidence)

- ______________________________
- ______________________________
- ______________________________

What are the interesting details?

- ______________________________
- ______________________________
- ______________________________

What is my question?

- ______________________________

____

____

____

What's important?

- ______________________________

____

____

Academic vocabulary:

- ______________________________
- ______________________________
- ______________________________

Words or pictures of interesting words I did not understand:

- ______________________________
- ______________________________
- ______________________________

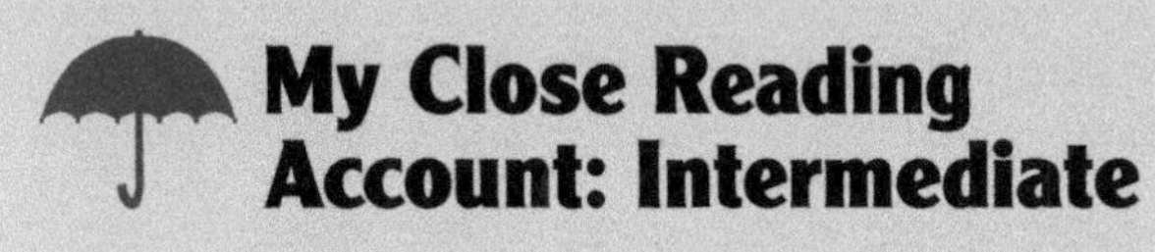

My Close Reading Account: Intermediate

Name: ______________________ Date: ______

Title: ______________________________

Author: ______________________________

How many times did I read this text? ______

What is my purpose for reading?

____

____

____

What is my purpose for writing?

____

____

____

What surprised me in the text?

____

____

Academic vocabulary:

- ______________________________
- ______________________________

Interesting words:

- ______________________________
- ______________________________

E-I-Q-T strategy for both fiction and nonfiction

Evidence (events for fiction and facts for nonfiction)

Ideas for building argument

Questions

Theme/importance

What did I learn? (cite evidence)

- ______________________________

  Page ______________

- ______________________________

  Page ______________

- ______________________________

  Page ______________

Ideas for building argument:

- ______________________________
- ______________________________

What is my question?

- ______________________________

____

What's important?

- ______________________________

____

____

My Close Reading Account: Upper Grades

Name: ______________________ Date: ______

Title: ________________________________

Author: ______________________________

How many times did I read this text? _______

What is my purpose for reading?

____

____

____

Things that surprised me (with page numbers):

- ________________________________

  Page ____________________

- ________________________________

  Page ____________________

Questions I had during reading:

____

____

Confusing or unknown key words or phrases:

- ________________________________

  Page ____________________

- ________________________________

  Page ____________________

- ________________________________

  Page ____________________

Question-Answer-Relationship (QAR) questions:

- ________________________________

  Page ____________________

- ________________________________

  Page ____________________

- ________________________________

  Page ____________________

- ________________________________

  Page ____________________

Ideas for building argument:

- ________________________________

  Page ____________________

- ________________________________

  Page ____________________

Key ideas/major points for this text:

- ________________________________

  Page ____________________

- ________________________________

  Page ____________________

What was the author's purpose for writing?

____

____

____

____

Maupin House *by*

capstone®

professional

At Maupin House by Capstone Professional, we continue to look for professional development resources that support grades K–8 classroom teachers in areas, such as these:

Literacy	Language Arts
Content-Area Literacy	Research-Based Practices
Assessment	Inquiry
Technology	Differentiation
Standards-Based Instruction	School Safety
Classroom Management	School Community

If you have an idea for a professional development resource, visit our Become an Author website at:
http://maupinhouse.com/index.php/become-an-author

There are two ways to submit questions and proposals.

1. You may send them electronically to:
   http://maupinhouse.com/index.php/become-an-author

2. You may send them via postal mail. Please be sure to include a self-addressed stamped envelope for us to return materials.

Acquisitions Editor
Capstone Professional
1 N. LaSalle Street, Suite 1800
Chicago, IL 60602